Also by Burton L. White:

*The First Three Years of Life*
New and Revised

# Raising a Happy, Unspoiled Child

## BURTON L. WHITE

SIMON & SCHUSTER

New York   London   Toronto   Sydney   Tokyo   Singapore

**SIMON & SCHUSTER**
Rockefeller Center
1230 Avenue of the Americas
New York, New York 10020

Designed by Irving Perkins Associates, Inc.

Manufactured in the United States of America

10  9  8  7  6  5  4  3  2  1

Library of Congress Cataloging-in-Publication Data

White, Burton L., date.
    Raising a happy, unspoiled child / Burton L. White.
        p.    cm.
    Includes  bibliographical references and index.
    1. Child rearing. 2. Parenting.  I. Title.
HQ769. W514              1994
649'.1--dc20                              94-7838
                                          CIP

ISBN: 0-671-79661-5

*To Janet Hodgson-White and her father, Robert Hodgson,
with gratitude, admiration, and love*

# Acknowledgments

My career studying how children develop has now spanned some thirty-six years. I am in debt to far too many people to list. I certainly have to cite those who contributed directly to this book. My wife and colleague, Janet Hodgson-White, deserves first mention. She worked with me in our model program of parent education since it began. Her dedication was unflagging, but more than that, her observations and suggestions contributed significantly to my understanding.

Our other colleagues, Marjorie Correia, Terry Glick, and my daughter Emily, have also made substantial contributions. I owe a huge debt to the families we work with. I had no idea at the start how much we were to learn about the socialization process. I am also grateful to my editor, Gail Winston, for her enthusiastic reception of the concept of the book and for first-rate editing work.

—Burton L. White
Waban, Massachusetts

# Contents

PREFACE                                                                    17

INTRODUCTION                                                               21

THE BASIS FOR THE INFORMATION IN THIS BOOK                                 23

THE EIGHT SPECIAL SOCIAL ABILITIES OF THE
    DELIGHTFUL SIX-YEAR-OLD                              31

THE NINE DISTINGUISHING NONSOCIAL ABILITIES OF
    THE WELL-DEVELOPED SIX-YEAR-OLD                       32

EARLY CONCLUSIONS ABOUT SOCIAL DEVELOPMENT                                 36


CHAPTER 1
BIRTH TO FIVE AND ONE-HALF MONTHS                                          49

NORMAL SOCIAL DEVELOPMENT                                                  49

THE DEVELOPMENT OF INTEREST IN PEOPLE                                      50

THE EMERGENCE OF SOCIAL AWARENESS—THE TICKLE                               51

THE DEVELOPMENT OF SPECIAL SOCIAL ABILITIES                                52

THE DEVELOPMENT OF A SOCIAL STYLE                                          52

HOW A NEWBORN'S PRINCIPAL ASSETS FUNCTION
    TOGETHER DURING THE FIRST MONTHS OF LIFE             53

THE THREE OUTCOMES OF A BABY'S DISCOMFORT                                  54

CALL ME IRRESISTIBLE                                                       55

WHAT CAN GO WRONG? NOT MUCH                                                59

*Neglected Babies Don't Become Spoiled*                                    64

How to Raise a Delightful Child      64
     *Goals—Social Characteristics of a Delightful*
         *Three-Year-Old*      64
Comforting a Very Young Baby      66
     *Using a Pacifier*      67
     *The Elevator Move*      68
     *Gentle Movement Through Space*      68
     *The Automobile Ride*      69
     *Various Sound Patterns*      69
Sometimes You Will Fail      71
The Impact of Colic      71
Having Fun with Your Baby      72
Signs of the Beginning of a New Stage of
     Development—The Emergence of the
     Intentional Cry      73


CHAPTER 2
FIVE AND ONE-HALF
TO SEVEN AND ONE-HALF MONTHS      74

Normal Social Development: The Development of
     Interest in People      74
     *Early Stranger Anxiety*      74
The Development of Special Social Abilities      76
     *The Ability to Get Attention in Socially Acceptable Ways*      76
     *The Intentional Cry for Company*      76
     *The Intentional Cry and Spoon Feeding*      77
What to Do When There Is Nothing to Do      78
The Development of a Social Style      82
     *The Emergence of the Capacity to Complain*      82
How Things Can Go Wrong—Pay Close Attention      83
Doing the Job Well      85
     *Goals*      85
     *What to Do*      85
     *The Key—Knowing What Interests a Baby and*
         *Designing a Suitable Environment*      87

*How to Handle Sleep Situations*     93

SUMMARY     95

SIGNS THAT A NEW STAGE IS BEGINNING: THE EMERGENCE
OF THE ABILITY TO GET ACROSS A ROOM ON HIS OWN     96

CHAPTER 3
SEVEN AND ONE-HALF TO FOURTEEN MONTHS     97

NORMAL SOCIAL DEVELOPMENT     97

NATURE VERSUS NURTURE     98

THE DEVELOPMENT OF INTEREST IN PEOPLE     98

*Stranger Anxiety*     98

*Separation Anxiety*     99

*Sibling Rivalry*     100

THE DEVELOPMENT OF SPECIAL SOCIAL ABILITIES     101

*Using an Adult as a Resource*     103

*Expressing Feelings, Both Positive and Negative,*
*Toward an Adult*     103

*Showing Pride in Achievement*     103

*Engaging in Make-Believe or Pretend Play*     104

THE DEVELOPMENT OF A SOCIAL STYLE     105

*Three Critical Social Lessons*     105

Learning About the Effects of Varying Degrees of
Crying     105

Acquiring Habits—Good and Bad     111

Imitation     114

Learning to Insist on Getting One's Way     117

*The Remarkable Significance of What the Nine- to*
*Twelve-Month-Old Learns During Diapering*     119

*The Balance Among Principal Interests*     120

HOW THE PROCESS CAN GO WRONG     123

*How the Interest in People Can Get Out of Hand*     124

*What Kind of Parenting Style Do You Adopt When*
*Your Baby Learns to Crawl?*     124

WHY THE DEVELOPMENT OF SPECIAL SOCIAL ABILITIES
IS NOT AT RISK AT THIS POINT     129

Contents

HOW AN UNDESIRABLE SOCIAL STYLE BEGINS TO FORM    129

*Crying After a Minor Accident*    130

*The Development of Bad Habits*    131

*How Learning to Insist on Having Your Way Can*
*Get Out of Hand*    132

Insisting on Getting Your Way When It Is Time to
Go to Sleep    132

The First Struggle for Power    133

SUMMARY    133

A SURPRISING AND IMPORTANT FACT ABOUT
EXPLANATIONS AND THE SEVEN- AND ONE-HALF
TO FOURTEEN-MONTH-OLD CHILD    136

HOW TO GUIDE YOUR BABY THROUGH THE FIRST
DIFFICULT STAGE OF SOCIAL DEVELOPMENT    138

*Goals*    138

*1) Maintaining the Balance Among the Primary*
*Interests*    139

Safety-Proofing the Home    140

Allowing Exploration of as Much of the Home as
Possible    141

*2) Teaching a Child to Take Minor Difficulties in Stride*    142

*3) Preventing the Development of Bad Habits*    143

Discipline: Getting Rid of a Bad Habit—Restriction of
Movement    145

*4) Teaching a Child He Has a Limited Right to Insist on*
*Getting His Way or to Repeat Something to Make Sure*
*He Was Understood*    147

Diapering: A Golden Opportunity    148

How to Diaper a Baby with a Minimum of Fuss While
at the Same time Teaching Her a Valuable Lesson
About Living in Her Family    148

A Second Classic Opportunity—Responding to
Overtures    149

Sleep: A Special Case    150

Setting Limits: The Need to Take the Baby's Point of
View into Account    151

A Milder Form of Learning to Insist—Initiating
    Games    153
SUMMARY    154
SIGNS THAT A NEW STAGE OF SOCIAL DEVELOPMENT IS
    BEGINNING    156

CHAPTER 4
FOURTEEN TO TWENTY-TWO TO THIRTY
MONTHS—A PREVIEW OF ADOLESCENCE    158

NORMAL SOCIAL DEVELOPMENT    158
THE DEVELOPMENT OF INTEREST IN PEOPLE    159
    *The Social Basis for the Appeal of Balls and Books*    159
    *Do Babies This Age Need to Spend Time with*
        *Other Toddlers?*    160
    *Sibling Rivalry*    162
THE DEVELOPMENT OF SPECIAL SOCIAL ABILITIES    164
THE DEVELOPMENT OF A SOCIAL STYLE    166
    *From Initiating Games to Directing Activities*    166
THE BALANCE AMONG THE PRIMARY INTERESTS    168
THE COMPLAINING/HAPPINESS INDEX    168
THE MANY SOCIAL LESSONS TODDLERS LEARN    172
WHEN THINGS GO WRONG    173
    *The Emergence of the Capacity to Bully*    175
    *Three Major Consequences of Poor Socialization*
    *During the Seven-and-One-Half-to-Twenty-two-Month*
    *Period*    179
HOW TO GUIDE YOUR CHILD THROUGH THE MOST
    DIFFICULT STAGE OF SOCIAL DEVELOPMENT—
    FOURTEEN TO TWENTY-TWO MONTHS    180
THE GOAL—THE BENEFITS OF RAISING AN ABSOLUTELY
    WONDERFUL, HAPPY, SECURE, AND SOCIALLY
    EFFECTIVE TWENTY-TWO-MONTH-OLD CHILD    181
HOW TO RAISE AN ABSOLUTELY WONDERFUL
    TWENTY-TWO-MONTH-OLD CHILD    185
    *Experimenting with Power*    185

*Prevention of Proximity—A Humane Way to Control
      a Fourteen- to Twenty-two-Month-Old Child*            188
   *Prevention of Proximity Versus "Time Out"*               190
MAINTAINING THE BALANCE AMONG THE PRIMARY
   INTERESTS                                                 192
   *The Special Potential of Puzzles*                        192
   *Part-Time Versus Full-Time Parenting*                    194
SUMMARY                                                      195
SIGNS THAT A NEW STAGE OF SOCIAL DEVELOPMENT
   IS BEGINNING                                              196


CHAPTER 5

TWENTY-TWO TO THIRTY TO THIRTY-SIX
MONTHS—A PERIOD OF INCREDIBLE
ENJOYMENT OR INCREASING STRESS                               197

NORMAL SOCIAL DEVELOPMENT                                    197
THE DEVELOPMENT OF INTEREST IN PEOPLE                        198
   *The Direction of Social Interest*                        200
THE DEVELOPMENT OF SPECIAL SOCIAL ABILITIES                  201
THE DEVELOPMENT OF A SOCIAL STYLE                            205
   *Testing—An Important Indicator*                          205
WHEN THINGS HAVE NOT GONE WELL—A CHRONIC
   TUG OF WAR                                                209
WHEN THE PROCESS HAS GONE WELL AFTER
   TWENTY-TWO TO TWENTY-FOUR MONTHS                          214
   *What to Do About Nursery School*                         214


CHAPTER 6

SPECIAL TOPICS                                               216

PRINCIPAL HAZARDS TO WATCH OUT FOR                           216
   *Special Concerns About the Baby's Health*                216
   *Prematurity*                                             217
   *Late Parenting*                                          218

| | |
|---|---|
| *Chronic Illness* | 219 |
| *Prolonged Colic* | 219 |
| OTHER COMMON OBSTACLES | 220 |
| *Guilt* | 220 |
| *Adoption* | 221 |
| *Parent's Temperament* | 222 |
| *Common Conditions That Make It Difficult to Satisfy a* | |
| *Baby's Curiosity and Motor Interests* | 226 |
| WHAT ABOUT GRANDPARENTS? | 230 |
| TRIPS—GO NOW, PAY LATER | 231 |
| THE EFFECTS OF A NANNY OR AN AU PAIR ON YOUR | |
| CHILD'S SOCIAL DEVELOPMENT | 231 |
| SOCIAL DEVELOPMENT AND HAPPINESS | 233 |
| A FINAL NOTE—BE CAUTIOUS | 235 |
| | |
| CHAPTER 7 | |
| CONCLUDING REMARKS | 237 |
| | |
| RECOMMENDED READINGS | 239 |
| INDEX | 243 |

# Preface

When I wrote my first book, some twenty-three years ago, I did so with a fair amount of apprehension. After all, I had never written a book before. The result was a slim monograph for graduate students that reported the results of my first independent research with babies during their first six months of life.

My second book, which followed just two years later, was the first of three reports on a large and expensive research study I was directing called the Harvard Preschool Project (1965–1978). At that time I was directing a staff of seventeen people, all focused on one question: "How do experiences affect the development of a child's abilities during the first six years of life?" The findings of that research have been of central importance for all the work I have done since. At that time, like any person directing a sizable research venture, I was obliged to report quickly and regularly on our findings. That book was written to further science, and frankly, my own and my colleagues' academic careers. Like the first, it was not written for popular consumption, but rather for other researchers interested in the subject of human development, and for college courses.

My third book was *The First Three Years of Life,* written in 1974. I was very excited at the prospect of writing that book. Having already spent nine years directing a huge, unprecedented research project and having the joy of observing a large number of parents and children in everyday situations—in homes, on playgrounds, and in nursery schools—I was certain I could help parents and their babies. What a privilege! What an exhilarating prospect!

*The First Three Years of Life* has been in print continuously since 1975. Now in its third edition, it has been published in nine foreign countries and read by millions of people. The success of that book and, in particular, the fact that so many families have found it helpful in raising their children have been enormously gratifying.

My second book for general readers, published a few years later, was called *A Parent's Guide to the First Three Years of Life.* It listed the most common questions parents had asked me since the publication of *The First Three Years,* along with my answers. The book was a good idea, but it certainly did not represent an exciting conceptual breakthrough.

And now we come to this book. Once again I am very excited, for I am sure that a large percentage of parents, particularly those expecting or raising their first child, will find solid help here. From my travels around the country and my intensive work with families in our New Parents as Teachers program, I know how widespread the need is for a book to help parents avoid raising an unpleasant, overly self-centered three-year-old child. Repeatedly, we have found it essential to counsel parents that they will have much less trouble nourishing the intellectual abilities of their child than they will with developing the social skills that create a child who will be a pleasure to live with. It has been my observation that few experiences in life bring the joy that the secure, socially capable three-year-old gives to parents. This book can help you achieve that wondrous outcome. What that means is that the typical difficulties that occur during the inevitable negativistic period of the second year of life will be reduced. During the third year of life, the very unpleasant behaviors characteristic of a spoiled, tantrum-throwing child will be virtually nonexistent. Your two-year-old won't struggle with you. Your child will be delighted with life just about all the time and will find it much easier than it might have been to form her first friendships. Finally, you will have started your child on a solid path toward developing into a secure, loving adult. Realizing only a modest fraction of these benefits wouldn't be a bad return for a few hours of reading, so read on.

# Introduction

ABOUT two years ago, one little boy made a special impression on me. Because his family was participating in our New Parents as Teachers program, I was able to watch Dennis develop from shortly after his birth until the end of his twenty-sixth month. At five months of age he was already very special. He had a glorious smile, which he flashed with great effect to everyone. Though not at all handsome, he had a dynamic, vivacious quality that was totally endearing. Clearly, he was very happy to be alive!

At two years of age, Dennis had turned into an extremely unpleasant tormentor of his parents and his younger brother. In a home visit I made at that time, he provoked his father continuously throughout the hour I spent with them. We spent the time in their kitchen, and Dennis very quickly began to demonstate that he knew exactly where to go and what to do to get immediate attention from his dad. He went to the water cooler and started pressing the button to drain the water. It was obvious that many such episodes had preceded this one and that Dennis already had been scolded repeatedly about this behavior. So he was not at all surprised when his father told him to stop what he was doing; indeed, he clearly expected this response. Clearly, he had trained his father well.

No sooner was Dennis pulled away from the water

cooler than he moved to the table where his six-month-old brother was lying in an infant seat. Confident his father was watching him, Dennis took a poke at his brother and, sure enough, his father yelled at him to stop. I'm quite sure that if his father had ignored him, he would have been puzzled and would have poked his brother again.

Dennis's next target was a kitchen cabinet, where he began to smear food on the door. During each step of this routine, he was scolded and partially restrained by his embarrassed (and harassed) father, but he would hesitate only momentarily before taking off in the direction of more mischief. His knowledge of ways to get his father to pay attention to him was vast. He knew every button to push. Such behavior requires a good mind, but that's not much consolation to a parent who has to put up with the behavior day after day.

This kind of pattern of rapid, sequential annoyances is not at all unusual in the third year of life. It usually surfaces at about twenty months and grows steadily in the weeks that follow. By twenty-four months of age many children have honed the process into virtuoso form.

I have absolutely no doubt as to how this wonderful five-month-old developed into a really unpleasant two-year-old. I had a ringside seat. I watched it happen, and have no doubt either about how it happened or how it could have been prevented. By no means was it inevitable.

When I read analyses of the so-called "difficult" child, examples such as that of the two-year-old Dennis come to mind. I have no doubt about the existence of inborn factors that contribute to the development of personality. My staff and I, however, have been privileged to watch the personalities of substantial numbers of children take shape during their early years of life, especially during the period between eight and twenty-four months, during which the more important effects of experience can easily be seen.

Parents living with a three-year-old who is causing them grief may find comfort in an explanation of their child's distressing behavior that focuses on inborn temperamental qualities. I wish I could go along with such a position, but I can't. I honestly believe that with very few exceptions, the common, extremely unpleasant behaviors of those three-year-olds we call "spoiled" were unknowingly taught to them by parents who loved them.

These are the children for whom the phrase the "terrible twos" was coined. An unspoiled child, on the other hand, does not have tantrums after his second birthday, except under extraordinary circumstances. Such a child will be happy most of the time, whereas the spoiled two-year-old will regularly find lots to complain about.

## THE BASIS FOR THE INFORMATION IN THIS BOOK

It is very important for any reader of a book about babies and how to raise them to be well informed about the basis for the statements, descriptions, and recommendations offered. A peculiar and quite important quality of the field of parent education is that a wide variety of authors have written about the subject of raising babies. Among others, the list includes pediatricians, psychologists, social workers, parents, and grandparents. What they all have in common is an interest in helping parents provide the best possible experiences for their new children. All, therefore, focus on recommendations for the best parenting practices.

An interesting question arises: "How does an author become qualified to give advice on parenting practices?" Can you become an expert by raising one or more children? Not likely.* It is so hard to be objective about one's own children. Then, too, how many can you raise? Not enough.

---

*A conspicuous exception is the work of Jean Piaget, the Swiss genetic epistemologist. I, along with many others, think that his research on the development of intelligence is the finest every done on the subject. It was performed with only three subjects—his own children! Piaget was a genius, but, alas, as far as I can tell, the only genius in this field.

Can you become an expert on parenting by engaging in pediatric practice? At first glance, this looks like a more promising route, and some of the most widely used books on child-rearing have been written by pediatricians. But aside from medical school, a pediatrician's principal source of knowledge about parenting is the well-baby examination. True, physicians hear a fair amount from mothers about what is like to be a parent during the typical fifteen minutes of discussion following a physical examination. They may also pick up additional information through reading. And, of course, a modest amount of attention is given to the topic in medical school. Interestingly, however, and more to the point, direct exposure to the ongoing process of parenting is not a part of pediatricians' training or their practice. Furthermore, their visits to the home are exceedingly rare, and when they do take place, these visits do not focus on parenting. My irreverent conclusion, then, is that most, if not all, pediatricians are not well qualified to write books on how to raise young children. Keeping a baby healthy? Yes. Monitoring growth? Yes. But guiding language development? Or knowing what to look for as the baby acquires social skills? Or guiding which methods of discipline to use as the infant evolves rapidly during the first years? Unfortunately, no.

Another indication of how shaky the basis for parenting advice can be is an experience I had last year. The Center for Parent Education, a small nonprofit agency I direct, was hired by a state department of education to provide in-service training for about seventy family educators. The supervisor of the various programs involved was aware of the possibility that her entire staff of workers might not have had fully adequate training in child development. My associates and I were to provide an intensive week of work.

In order to get a sense of where to start, I created a simple ten-item multiple-choice test. My plan was to administer the test at the beginning of the week and again when we finished.

Here are four items from the test:

1. Children first begin to become mobile (move around on their own) at:
   a. Three months
   b. Five months
   c. Seven months
   d. Nine months
2. What is the average age at which children say their first words?
   a. Five months
   b. Eight months
   c. Fourteen months
   d. Eighteen months
3. What is the average age at which children understand their first words?
   a. Five months
   b. Eight months
   c. Fourteen months
   d. Eighteen months
4. How long after babies can climb upstairs can they come downstairs safely?
   a. One day
   b. Two weeks
   c. One month
   d. Two months

As you can see, these questions deal with simple, basic information. Nothing fancy; nothing technical.

Since there were four choices available for each question, someone knowing nothing about babies could get a score of 25 percent on the basis of chance alone. Allowing for some disagreements about the correct answers, you might expect an experienced person who provides parent education to families to answer at least two-thirds of the questions correctly.

The average score for this group was 35 percent. I was

somewhat surprised, but not dramatically so. Since 1976 my colleagues and I have held training seminars throughout the country that have been attended by over 25,000 professionals from education, medicine, social work, and related fields. I can assure you that this limited knowledge of basic facts is a widespread phenomenon. The problem is not limited to practitioners. Someone trained these people and someone wrote the books they read during their training.

In my judgment, to acquire genuinely useful, accurate information about parenting, no substitute exists for direct, systematic study of the process. Unfortunately, until very recently next to no work of that kind has been done. Even today, when it comes to the first two to three years of life, the parenting process usually occurs in the home. True, parents and babies do make occasional excursions out of the home, and substitute care, with increasing numbers of infants doing a lot of growing up out of their homes, does happen. However, if you want to know what parenting is like, there simply is no substitute for going to homes. You have to observe the ordinary actions of parents, in a systematic and accurate way.

Furthermore, it is obvious to anybody who seriously studies human development that one, two, three, or even four exposures to the parenting process in a home is nowhere near adequate. Why? Simply because when parents are being observed their behavior is always affected by the presence of the observer. At first, most parents try to get their baby to demonstrate her many talents. Some parents feel uncomfortable or nervous. So far, we have not figured out how to avoid completely what is known as the "observer effect." If, however, observations take place repeatedly over many months, the behavior of parents seems gradually to become more natural and less strained.

Two other common approaches to the study of child-rearing practices are the interview and survey methods, which use questionnaires. Both are quick and inexpensive, but I don't have much faith in them. Parents find it very difficult to be candid about certain subjects, such as sibling rivalry. When we asked a mother of a three-year-old how the child felt about her eighteen-month-old younger brother, we were told, "Alexandra loves her brother. They play together so well! At times, however, it seems as if she doesn't know her own strength." We had been observing Alexandra and her brother at home, on a regular basis. It was clear that Alexandra regularly used all the strength she had in alternately trying to hurt her baby brother and protecting herself from his increasing aggressiveness. I think the subject was somewhat embarrassing for their mother. By the way, Alexandra's behavior toward her baby brother is what we have seen in comparable circumstances in hundreds of homes, with very few exceptions.

If you want to acquire really solid information about the effects of various methods of discipline, you have to go to many homes and watch what happens when different approaches are tried with many children, in different family configurations and over many months. If you want to learn when children begin to watch television, you have to observe, in their homes, many children of different ages, over many months, to see when they actually begin to look at the set. Asking parents for such information is surely easier, but don't count on it to be accurate.

The background for this book had its beginnings more than forty years ago when, in 1952, I made a decision to change careers. At that time I was in the army, working as a mechanical engineer. For many reasons, I decided to change my focus from machines to people. In particluar, I decided to address my energies to the question of where solid, caring people came from. The Greek philosopher Plato wrote that competence and goodness were related. He wrote that a capable person was more likely to be a kind person than was a person of limited ability. That notion always made sense to me, in spite of the fact that many conspicuous exceptions exist.

After leaving the army in 1953, I sought additional

education, first in philosophy, then in psychology. Psychology as a discipline was clearly more appropriate than philosophy for my interest in trying to understand more about how well-developed people got that way. On the other hand, I was struck by the remarkable orientation toward pathology in the field of psychology as it pertained to studies of development. In the 1950s, the principal theories in the area of personality and motivation derived from the work of Sigmund Freud. Reading the ideas of other outstanding theorists such as Harry Stack Sullivan and Erik Erikson was exciting and provocative. Yet something about the material left me unsatisfied.

When I finally began to learn about what in those days was called ego psychology, I found ideas that seemed more suited to my particular interest. Ego psychologists studied human strengths and psychological health rather than how to deal with neuroses. I was very much impressed by the work of Robert White of Harvard and Abraham Maslow of Brandeis University. Maslow so impressed me in his writings on the subject of "self-actualized" people that at the first opportunity I transferred my graduate studies to his program at Brandeis.

Whereas major thinkers such as Freud evolved their ideas about how people develop from their therapeutic work with patients in difficulty, Maslow took an opposite tack. He argued that in order for a scientific approach to human development to be sound, one had to study the lives of exemplary individuals as well as those in trouble. His subjects therefore included people like Albert Schweitzer, Eleanor Roosevelt, Mahatma Gandhi, and even Jesus Christ. After identifying a person as outstanding, Maslow would analyze what stood out in their various characteristic behaviors and qualities. I was excited by both his focus and his research approach. Eight years later, it was his examination of the lives of outstanding people that shaped the early work of the Harvard Preschool Project. The outstanding people I began to look at, however, were only six years old.

In 1957 I began my research on babies while working on a Ph.D. in psychology at Brandeis University That research, which focused on infants between birth and six months of age, continued until I was awarded my degree in 1960 and for some eight years afterward. I focused on the role of experience in the development of the very first abilities of babies.

Those of us interested in human development owe a huge debt of gratitude to the leaders of the American civil rights movement for their activities during the late 1950s and early 1960s. In my opinion, their insistent demands for more government action in the early education of children from poor families broke open the whole subject of learning and development (and child-rearing) in the first years of life. Spokespeople for low-income families pointed out that one of the great features of America was that you could be born poor and still make a good life for yourself and your family through educational achievement. Yet, they noted, too few children from low-income families did well in education. Drop-out rates were high. Going on to college was less likely than for children of the more privileged classes. Noting that poor educational achievement was often apparent when children began school at five or six years of age, they demanded that the government do something about school readiness. The result was the creation of Project Headstart.

Soon after Headstart began, *Sesame Street* was initiated. It was sold on the basis that television could become a potent tool to assist the Headstart teacher. Whether it succeeded in that task or not, it certainly helped raise the level of consciousness of parents and many others about the significance of early learning, both in the United States and in many other parts of the world.

A result of that dramatic increase in interest in preschool learning was that, for the first time in history, huge amounts of money became available for research on the development of the child between birth and six years of age. Those resources made it possible for me to begin the

Harvard Preschool Project in 1965. The Preschool Project was—and remains—unique. Seventeen people, working under my direction, set about to understand how experiences in the first six years of life affect readiness for formal education. We wanted to learn how to help a child become "educable." After a few years, we began to refer to our goal as the development of "the competent" six-year-old.

One of our earliest tasks was to define what we meant by a competent or well-developed six-year-old child. The usual practice in child development research was to examine through a literature search what had already been established about a given subject. We assigned people to scour research reports of all kinds to find recorded descriptions of the qualities of well-developed six-year-old children. We were very surprised to learn that there were no such records anywhere. Some hints as to what we had hoped to find were in the pioneering work of Lois Murphy. Murphy and her colleagues had written two books on three- to five-year-old children they had been studying at Sarah Lawrence College. One of those books described their method of study, while the other provided a detailed history of one very nicely developed little boy. Otherwise, our search came up empty. We decided the only thing we could do was generate our own definition of a nicely developed six-year-old child.

It was at this point that we applied Maslow's approach. We made arrangements with families and schools to observe substantial numbers of three- to six-year-old children in order to find the one child in thirty whom everyone would agree was indisputably a "competent" six-year-old child. I made it clear to everyone that I was interested in children who were outstanding in their social abilities as well as in their intelligence and use of language. (We took pains to avoid including in our group of competent children the occasional child who was obviously extremely bright but didn't do well socially.)

Once we had gained access to a broad range of groups

of children, we began systematic observations of their day-to-day behaviors. My staff and I repeatedly watched children from many kinds of families over a nine-month period in several settings—at preschools, in kindergartens, on playgrounds, and in their own homes. We came to a unanimous agreement on the characteristics in the behavior of wonderful six-year-olds that most distinguished them from average and below-average children of the same age. We were struck by how certain social behaviors stood out. These wonderful children were clearly different when it came to the way they interacted with other children and adults. Of course, they weren't totally different, but the degree to which their social abilities had developed was always noticeably greater than that of their peers.

## THE EIGHT SPECIAL SOCIAL ABILITIES OF THE DELIGHTFUL SIX-YEAR-OLD

### With Adults

A wide variety of socially acceptable, effective
   attention-getting methods.
The ability to express feelings, both positive and
   negative, to adults.
Pride in achievement. They know they have
   talent.
The ability to use an adult as a resource, having
   first determined they cannot achieve a goal on
   their own.
The tendency to engage in make-believe or
   role-play activities.

### With Peers

The ability to both lead and follow another child.
The ability to express feelings, both positive and
   negative, to another child.

The tendency to be competitive and to know what
a "good job" is.

Those eight distinguishing characteristics, as seen in social interchanges, have for the most part stood up well over many years of research and parent-education work. Personnel familiar with three- to six-year-old children consistently confirm the accuracy of this picture.

In addition to the social characteristics that we identified as especially well developed in outstanding six-year-olds, a collection of nonsocial abilities were, of course, noted as well.

## THE NINE DISTINGUISHING NONSOCIAL ABILITIES OF THE WELL-DEVELOPED SIX-YEAR-OLD

Good language development.
The ability to notice small details or discrepancies.
The ability to anticipate consequences.
The ability to deal with abstractions.
The ability to put yourself in the place of another.
The ability to make interesting associations.
The ability to carry out complicated activities.
The ability to use resources effectively.
Dual focusing—being able to maintain focus on a
task while simultaneously keeping track of what
is taking place around her.

A discussion of these nonsocial qualities can be found in *The First Three Years of Life.* To some extent they'll be referred to in later sections of this book as they relate to the socialization process.

The Preschool Project not only had a large number of personnel, it also had a very broad scope. While social abilities forced themselves into our work early on, and remained a conspicuous part of it, they were only one of several major foci of the work. In our observations we used stopwatches to time the many different kinds of experiences children underwent. While we tried to build a complete picture of the moment-to-moment behaviors and surrounding circumstances of young children, we were also very much interested in the evolution of their interests, and, of course, we paid a good deal of attention to the many abilities they showed as they grew.

A major turning point in our research effort came as a result of our examination of the emergence of this seventeen-item picture of excellent functioning in the six-year-old child. After examining our records on children between two and one-half and six years of age, we agreed that the pattern of behaviors characteristic of the outstanding six-year-old could be found in children as young as three years of age. What seemed to happen between the third and the sixth birthday was the refinement of this remarkable pattern of behavior rather than the emergence of additional distinguishing characteristics.

A conspicuous example of this refining process was the development of the ability to take the perspective of another person. In Piaget's pioneering work on mental function in children, the ability to see the world from the point of view of another person signaled the decline in egocentric thinking, the first form of thinking behavior. Piaget found that children routinely adopted what he called "socialized thought," in which they attempted to speak so that the listener would understand what they were saying. In contrast, egocentric thought principally serves the purpose of trying to satisfy the speaker's own needs. For a child to see things from another person's point of view requires that he replace egocentric thinking with socialized thought. Piaget reported that socialized thought generally surfaced when children were seven or eight years old, but we routinely found that form of behavior in our outstanding six-year-olds. Surprisingly, we usually found instances of socialized thought in our outstanding three-year-old group as well. But we never found all seventeen distinguishing characteristics in children less than three years of age.

As a result of our attempt to track the emergence of this highly desirable behavioral style, we came to an important conclusion: We felt that if we could learn something about how, under the best of circumstances, children arrived at this style by their third birthdays, we would have learned something of great value. Logically, looking at the first three years of life seemed to make the most sense as our next research task.

The notion of the special importance of the first three years of life was supported by the research of others as well. Large numbers of studies of psychological testing have clearly indicated that with certain groups of children, performance on intelligence and language tests at age three predicts ability levels of such children in later years. In particular, this statement applies to two groups of children, those who at age three are well advanced and those who were clearly behind the average child. In other words, the child at three with the language and intelligence of a child four years of age or older was very likely to be well above average at age six and therefore be well prepared to begin elementary school. On the other hand, the child who was nine months or more behind at age three on these two basic abilities was likely to fall further behind over the next few years and to be unprepared to begin formal education at age six.

In addition, a rich history of studies of child development pointed to uniquely important developments that took place during the first three years of life. The first of those developments was language acquisition. Students of the process unanimously agreed that most basic language capacity emerged by the third birthday. On average, the consensus was that two-thirds to three-quarters of all words to be used in ordinary conversation, throughout life, are usually understood by that age.

Students of social and emotional development were

equally convinced of the lasting significance of the impact of experiences during the first three years on a person's emotional well-being and capacity to form close relationships throughout life. Finally, the work of Piaget and others clearly indicated that the emergence of thinking ability took place toward the end of the second year, and that advances and delays of lasting significance often became apparent during the third year of life.

For all of these reasons, we decided that we simply had to concentrate on the development of children during the first three years of life.

In the late 1960s, performing research on the first three years of a child's life was very difficult. Group care for children of that age was not common. The approaches available to us were: interview data with parents, brief laboratory sessions with a baby, always accompanied by a parent, or work performed in the individual homes of children. I have never felt that interview data generated enough detail or that it was likely to produce accurate information. I also could never understand how one could study development in anywhere near adequate fashion by bringing a baby to the university. Rarely did that situation amount to more than one hour of contact. Piaget's pioneering work with his own three children struck me as being the soundest approach. That work featured a very large number of observations and experiments with his children, in their own home, over many months. This approach to complicated, lengthy developmental processes, called "process monitoring," is expensive, time-consuming, and laborious. Nonetheless, I believed then, and still do today, that it is the only suitable approach to the study of the development of a child during the first three years of life.

We observed dozens of families in their own homes once a month, from the time the babies were one until they were three years old. To get as accurate a picture as possible, observers took turns going into these homes.

We invested time and energy in trying to understand the

major differences in parenting styles associated with different outcomes in children. In addition, outstanding research by other students of early development required that we study related developmental processes, especially the growth of attachment between a child and her family.

This "naturalistic observation" phase of our work taught us a lot about the everyday lives of infants and their parents, and it allowed us to generate ideas about effective parenting practices.

The next step in the research process was to test some of our ideas with new families. Out of this experimental work came certain crude but potentially valuable conclusions about social development.

## EARLY CONCLUSIONS ABOUT SOCIAL DEVELOPMENT

It didn't take us very long to learn that delightful two-year-olds were marvelous people to have around. A two-year-old who has developed well is a great companion, a joy to talk with, full of humor, imagination, and originality. Just as obvious was the disturbing conclusion that unpleasant two-year-olds were quite common and, to put it midly, were no fun at all. Two-year-olds who complained much of the time each day were everywhere, as were aggressive two-year-olds who tended to hit other children routinely. Two-year-olds who engaged in a chronic tug of war with their mothers from morning till night were extremely common, along with two-year-olds who whined and cried and threw tantrums. Indeed, I can remember one woman who left town for two weeks to get away from her two-year-old. Many other parents would have joined her if only they could have.

In observing children from age two through age three, we learned that the child who was an extremely unpleasant person at two usually got worse as the months went by. You could count on such a child to become a tantrum thrower, especially in public places. Oh, how we felt for their parents! This already difficult situation was made considerably worse by the presence of a one-year-old brother or sister. Family after family told us that sibling rivalry was, by far, their worst ongoing problem. (Sibling rivalry was considerably less of a problem when the older child had been developing well.)

Tantrums and other forms of subcivil, downright nasty behaviors were almost never seen in the third year of life with those two-year-olds who had been developing wonderfully well. These were the children who were a pleasure to their parents. On the other hand, as delightful as such children were, they too quickly became jealous of a newly crawling younger sibling when the age gap between the children was less than three years.

These observations meant that (a) the "terrible twos" were indeed a reality, but (b) the "terrible twos" were not inevitable. Indeed, our conclusion then and now was very simple: The "terrible twos" are caused by overindulgence during the first two years of life.

We came to a few other basic, preliminary judgments during those early years of research. For example, we learned that most one-year-olds were very charming and agreeable. True, some of them demanded much more attention than others. Even when in perfect health, some one-year-old babies cried much more than others. They seemed to have a lot to complain about and made more demands to be picked up and held than others. We concluded that something involving overindulgence and spoiling began to show itself between the first and second birthdays. At that time, however, that was all we knew. We simply had no idea what went on during the first twenty-four months of life that led to the development of an impossible three-year-old.

We also noted (with amazement) that skillful manipulative behavior was quite common by thirteen or fourteen months of age. In particular, we observed that the whine was very often developed to a fine art by then. If a parent refused something that the baby wanted, the baby would often hesitate, look at his parent, and then produce a soft whine. The baby would then pause and look to see whether his parent gave in or not. If not, the baby would produce a slightly louder, more insistent, whine, pause once again, and look to see the effect. This routine could escalate through four or five repetitions to a pitch where the baby was screaming, at which point many a parent would simply fold and give the baby what he wanted. We marveled at the power, efficiency, and manipulative skill that had already developed in a child so tender in age and so small in stature. It was this common behavior that convinced me that the legendary "innocence of babes" is usually gone by fourteen months of age.

Sometime between fourteen and eighteen months of age, just about every baby we have ever observed entered into negativism, a stage where they seemed to be trying out their newly sensed interpersonal power. Once that stage began, we knew that trying to test a baby was going to be a problem. After all, the typical test used with young children consists of a series of harmless requests, such as "Where is the doggie?" or "Can you put the ball under the cup?" Many children between sixteen and eighteen months of age have the ability to deal with such test items, but they simply won't cooperate. Interestingly, his resistance is often especially evident if the baby's mother tries to help. Ordinarily, it is much easier to test a child who is under fourteen or over twenty-four months of age than one between fourteen and twenty-four months.

The ordinary social developments of the period between fourteen and twenty-four months of age seemed consistently to make it quite stressful for parents. Week by week babies seemed to get more and more ornery. This increase in willfulness happened with such regularity that we were certain that this transformation was of major significance for anyone raising a child. It is one reason I have maintained that few people do well being home full-time with even one such child. I have long advocated time away from one's own child during the fourteen- to twenty-four-month period. If a parent has to cope with two (or more) closely spaced children under three years of age, the need to have regular periods of time away from them is absolutely essential.

In talks to groups during the early 1970s, I very often pointed out how remarkably stressful life was for a full-time parent caring for two closely spaced children under the age of three once the younger one was a year and one-half old. I was then, and still remain, convinced that very few adults could successfully handle day-to day life with two such young children without lots of help. As observers, we were bowled over by the intensity and persistence of the stress in such situations. We wondered why this widespread, chronically painful situation wasn't more widely acknowledged. Surely women had been living under such conditions for a long time. Just as surely, if research in the home had been done earlier, any observer would have been equally impressed by its difficulties. Twenty years later, I am still struck by how difficult such circumstances are for full-time stay-at-home parents.

We also noted another consistent fact about social development during this time of life. Even when children ended up as absolutely delightful three-year-olds, their parents had to go through a minimum of six months of struggling with the child before the clouds parted and the sunshine returned.

Interestingly, parents often chose this particular time in their child's life to attempt to impose their will on their child with respect to certain classic situations. One of those situations involves pacifier use. Pacifiers are very commonly used during the first months of life, and I'm a strong advocate of their use. They can save parents and babies a great deal of irritation and stress. Some parents find that pressure is put on them by outsiders—sometimes friends, at other times grandparents—to wean the child from the pacifier. Very often this pressure begins when the child is between fourteen and twenty-four months of age.

A parallel situation is toilet training. In our experience, toilet training is most often (and easily) accomplished with first children sometime between the ages of two and two and one-half years. Many people, especially grandparents, believe that babies should be toilet-trained long before their second birthdays, and they let new parents know this in no uncertain terms.

Attempting to wean a fourteen- to twenty-four-month-old child from a pacifier or trying to get him to use a potty chair is not a good idea. Since you will have more than enough issues to dispute with your toddler, waiting a few months makes more sense.

During the early 1970s, when this general picture of social development was forming, I went through an experience that engraved itself indelibly upon my mind. It illustrated very clearly what could happen when overindulgence was a central feature of the parenting style. My wife and I were sitting in the waiting room of a health maintenance organization during the middle of a cold Boston winter. The room was rather large, with many benches, and could accommodate at least fifty people. The door opened and in walked a well-dressed mother and child, the woman perhaps in her early thirties, the child in his late twos. Both were dressed warmly. The woman pushed the child in his stroller over to an empty bench and then peeled off her own outer clothing. This done, she turned to her son and said, "Okay honey, let me take off some of those clothes so you can be more comfortable." The child, using absolutely minimal energy, glanced briefly at his mother and said elegantly, "No." His mother hesitated a moment and then said, "It's very warm in here, dear. If I don't take off your mittens and your hat and your jacket, you might get uncomfortable, maybe even sick." The child gave her a half second's attention and simply repeated, "No." The mother hesitated a moment before she patiently said, "Look, dear, all the other people here have their coats and jackets off. That's what we have to do because it's winter out and it's warm in here." Once again the child repeated his firm "No." My wife and I watched this episode go on and on over a period of at least ten minutes: the mother full of explanations and pleadings; the child making it plain that his decision was the controlling one, not hers, and that he was not going to accede to her wishes. Finally, after about fifteen minutes, she managed to get him to let her unbutton his jacket. That was as far as she could go.

No question of authority prevailed here. This two-and-one-half-year-old boy had clearly acquired a fair measure of authority over his mother. There are parents who seem to believe it is so important to encourage a child's independence of mind that they should be very careful about forcing their will on them. Others seem to be afraid that their two-and-one-half-year-old will throw a tantrum and cause them embarrassment. To this day, that incident sticks in my mind, even though I have seen many other examples of the same kind of parent-child relationship since then. As I have come to know many children who have developed in similar ways, I have noticed that these children also usually do not seem to be having as much fun as most two-and-one-half-year-olds.

What, then, were our major conclusions from the Harvard Preschool Project work from the period between the late 1960s and the mid-1970s?

1. Spoiling often surfaced by two years of age.
2. The "terrible twos" are not inevitable. Parents whose style was warm but firm had the best results. Parents who were warm and overindulgent usually had to suffer through the "terrible twos."
3. Negativism, self-assertion, and testing are all inevitable, beginning sometime between fourteen and eighteen months of life, and ending no sooner than six months after they begin.

4. The best parenting practices featured a consistently loving but firm hand by parents. The way we used to express it was to say, "Things go best when it is very clear to the child that the *parent* runs the home, *not* the baby."

5. Sibling rivalry problems should be expected when children are spaced less than three years apart. They are usually much worse when the older child has been spoiled.

All of these conclusions are described in *The First Three Years of Life,* first published in 1975. Following its publication, I regularly continued to do public speaking as well as research, staff training, and consulting at various places around the country. A very common question raised by audiences and letter writers was "What do you mean by 'be firm'? It's very well to advise parents to be firm, but unless you tell them how, you really leave them in trouble." At that time, many people thought that when I advocated firmness I meant that parents should have no reservations about spanking their child. Personally, the idea of anyone striking a two-and-one-half-year-old child bothered me a great deal. But throughout my professional career I have been most reluctant to make recommendations on parenting based on either my personal feelings or the experiences I've had with my own family. In order for a claim or recommendation to be justified, I have to be able to back it up with reasonably solid knowledge gained from research. Our extensive observations of children developing during their early years revealed that spanking, especially during a child's second and third year of life, was a common behavior on the part of most parents (who were invariably decent, caring people). It would have been very convenient if children developing poorly had received a great deal of spanking and those who were developing wonderfully had rarely or never been spanked. That, however, was not the case. I was left with a dilemma.

What I said to audiences and to correspondents was as follows: "I don't feel comfortable condemning spanking during the first three years of life. There certainly is no need at all for spanking in the first six or seven months of age. If, on the other hand, parents occasionally softly but firmly pat their children on the behind between seven months and two years of age, I simply cannot say that they're doing something harmful in view of what we've seen going on with successful families. Furthermore, it seems to me that an occasional modest pat on the behind is more likely to have the desired effect than the elaborate explanations we sometimes hear from parents who apparently believe that all interpersonal disagreements should be resolved using rational, civilized means, regardless of the age of the child."

That position was the only one I felt I could take as a professional, but I must confess I was not altogether comfortable with it. Since that time I have learned that there are alternative ways of controlling a child during the first years of life that don't require ever striking a child. Furthermore, these alternative methods are more effective than spanking. More about that later.

In 1977 the Westinghouse Corporation created a television version of *The First Three Years of Life* book called *The First Three Years*. Those programs are the most widely used audiovisual material in this country for parent education and staff training. At least one contribution to our work on avoiding a spoiled child came out of the making of that series. Each of the programs began with about ten minutes of a baby going about her natural behaviors in the home, followed by a discussion of children of that age with four or five couples. I remember clearly a sensible mother of a one-year-old who said something like the following: "I'm crazy about my daughter. I admire her spunk and I am delighted by her curiosity, *but* she does not have to play in my makeup." This particular statement really captured the essence of one major aspect of effective socializing, which we labeled "healthy selfishness." We have continued to use that concept since that time. It still rings true.

No doubt because I left the university in 1978 and didn't get involved with the New Parents as Teachers program in Missouri until 1981. I don't believe I made any significant progress between 1978 and 1982 in my understanding of the details of social development or the spoiling process. However, after a three-month planning period in the fall of 1981, my associates and I began to offer parent education and support to over 300 families at four locations in the state of Missouri under the auspices of the State Department of Education. I designed the New Parents as Teachers program (NPAT). This program built upon both the training we did at the Harvard Preschool Project in our experimental work and upon our first attempt to implement our ideas through the Brookline, Massachusetts, public schools in the early 1970s (the Brookline Early Education Project, or BEEP). After preliminary training of the core staff during the fall of 1981, the NPAT program began to serve families in January 1982.

For the next four years, I traveled to Missouri for three-day visits every six weeks. I would visit each of the four sites and go on home visits with each member of the staff. The entire staff and I would then meet to discuss how they were doing in implementing this unusual new program. Across the four sites, one particularily common concern was something that the home visitors were calling "overattachment" problems in children twelve to twenty-four months of age. It turned out that they were talking about children simply demanding an awful lot of attention from their parents. Going on home visits once every six weeks each time I visited Missouri did not allow me to delve very deeply into that particular problem. In retrospect, given what I have learned in the intervening years, I doubt that the recommendations I made back then did much good. I did believe that it was notable that this kind of problem was so common. It was not all that common in the Harvard Preschool Project work, although I certainly could recognize the symptoms. Since that time, it has turned out that this particular complaint on the part of parents has substantial significance.

I left the Missouri project in the fall of 1985, but it wasn't until 1989 that my understanding of social development during the first years of life began to expand. In the spring of 1989, my associates and I created a model NPAT program at the Center for Parent Education in Waban, Massachusetts. The Center is a nonprofit organization I established when I left Harvard in 1978. Soon after we started working with families, we found we simply couldn't avoid certain realities. Our attention was drawn to issues surrounding the social development of the children to a much greater degree than in our earlier work. Our parents were having no difficulty guiding their children toward outstanding levels of intelligence and language. The children were not having any difficulty learning to sit up, walk, or climb, either. Most of their difficulties involved social behaviors. Parents told us repeatedly that, above all, they wanted help in avoiding overindulging their children. The prospect of a spoiled child was something they dreaded.

In the last four years, working very closely with families, my associates and I have been able to fill in many of the details that describe the process by which a baby evolves from a newborn into the marvelously complex social creature that is a three-year-old child. We have provided monthly one-hour home visits with each of eighty families, beginning just before their babies were born and continuing until they were twenty-seven months old. We have also conducted ninety-minute group meetings with the same families every five to six weeks. In no way can I fully express the tremendous pleasure it has brought us to watch each new child take shape and become a complicated and fascinating individual. I am also quite delighted at how much we have learned about how the process takes place. The work is about as rewarding as anything I could imagine.

More than anything else, it has been our intensive

work with families in our ongoing model program that has led to this book. We now have a clear, detailed picture of how and why spoiling develops and, thank goodness, a solid (though not perfect) understanding of how to avoid it and how to guide a child toward a wonderful outcome at three years of age.

Few subjects are as important to and as valued by parents as the well-being and future of each new child. Our society does not train people to raise children, and the felt need for information is deep and widespread. Therefore a good deal of advice is offered year after year; books, articles, and pamphlets abound. Unfortunately, a lot of what becomes available is, plain and simply, useless or misleading.

As hard as it is to believe, it would appear that aside from the work that my associates and I have been involved in since 1965, no other study has ever been done of the month-to-month development of the young child or of the parenting process! While I'm sure our work contains many errors and omissions, I am equally sure that it is more firmly based in reality and more comprehensive and detailed than any other available information.

I have focused my research career on infant and early-childhood development for over thirty-six years. That doesn't guarantee that my perceptions are always accurate, but I certainly have done more baby watching than most people. I've been fortunate enough to be allowed to do sustained research (usually with many talented associates) in many kinds of homes. This research has featured bi-monthly observations of many children for up to two and one-half years. My colleagues and I have closely studied, in this manner, the development of hundreds of children. At the same time, I am obliged to point out that I and many others believe that the soundest knowledge of human development comes from research that uses reliable measures. Unfortunately, when it comes to the subject of social development, that kind of information is limited. In our work, we have measured what we could. We can advise you on sound, quantitative grounds that babies will start to use you as a resource (ask for help) between nine and one-half and eleven months of age. Similarly, we have good evidence that the typical twelve- to fifteen-month-old baby (at home) will approach a parent about ten times an hour in the course of a day. On the other hand, neither we nor anyone else has developed reliable measures for pride, self-confidence, and a host of other elements of a baby's social characteristics. Let me hasten to add that I firmly believe that what you'll find written in the following chapters is the best you can find anywhere and that you can count on it to be both practical and effective.

Helping parents guide their children's development in respect to the various major competencies such as language, intelligence, and sensory abilities is, of course, an important undertaking. We all want our children to make the most of their potential. But every parent that I have known wants their child to be happy and socially capable as well. Everything I have learned has convinced me that the experiences a child undergoes in her first three years of life constitute the major influences on the shaping of her social development. In other words, parents or whichever other adults are responsible for those early experiences are to a large extent shaping the personality of that new child. To the extent that there is truth in what I've been saying, this is both a heavy responsibility and a wonderful opportunity.

The pleasures that can be yours were perhaps most succinctly expressed by one mother in a group we worked with last year. In response to our usual questions about how things had been going with her twenty-two-month-old daughter, she said, "I want you to know I can't wait to get up in the morning to spend the day with her." It is my earnest hope that many of you who read this book will be able to make a comparable statement when your child becomes twenty-two months of age. I can assure you that a child who has stopped testing his parents by twenty-two to twenty-four months of age and who is happy and generally well developed is very likely to maintain those characteristics at least through the sixth birthday and very probably well beyond. If this book facilitates that outcome for you, I'll be very happy indeed, and so will you.

# CHAPTER 1

# Birth to
# Five and One-Half Months

## NORMAL SOCIAL DEVELOPMENT

THE story of the social development of each new baby is always fascinating. No one can predict what kind of person a newborn will become by her third birthday. What is most striking about every new baby is how helpless and needy she is. In contrast, the typical three-year-old is an impressively complicated and accomplished person. After watching the process take place hundreds of times, I still find excitement in watching each new child take shape. I can assure you that few experiences in your life will be more captivating than the one you are about to undergo.

The central focus of this book is how to raise an unspoiled child. That subject can be understood only within the larger context of social development. Three major social development strands are present from birth to the third birthday: the development of interest in people, the development of special social abilities, and the growth of a social style (or personality). In this chapter and those that follow, I will describe normal development, what can go wrong, and finally, what you can do at each stage to help your child become a delightful and capable three-year-old.

## THE DEVELOPMENT OF INTEREST IN PEOPLE

As far as I can tell, the normal newborn baby is totally oblivious to people. All that baby wants is to be comfortable. Your baby may glance at you briefly soon after birth, and during the next five or six weeks he may even stare at you at times. You may see something that looks like a small smile (not surprisingly, first-time parents see more of this than anyone else!). But only when your child becomes six to eight weeks of age, and her interest in looking at your face becomes unmistakable, will you realize how impersonal those early glances really were.

It is natural to think that attention to your face means that your baby knows you in some sense. The best evidence we have suggests that the amount of interest a two-month-old shows in any human face is more a function of the physical qualities of the face than it is of any budding feelings of love on the part of the baby. If a mother's facial characteristics feature low contrast, she may be somewhat disappointed for a short while in her baby's modest response to her. If her hair is light, her skin fair, and her eyes light green or blue, she may find that her dark-haired, fair-skinned, dark-eyed husband gets many more smiles from their baby. Not to worry; within a month the situation will change.

Once your baby reaches two and one-half months or so and her visual abilities mature, she begins to be able to see small nearby details clearly. She becomes a very reliable smiler, and everybody starts to have more fun. It also helps a lot that most babies begin to sleep for longer periods at night at about this time and everyone begins to feel more rested.

At two and one-half to three months of age, babies are

almost always very responsive and seem to like everybody. By three and one-half to four months of age, a very significant change takes place. Babies begin to smile more quickly and longer at the people who have been caring for them than at anyone else. They will continue to smile quite readily at just about anyone who presents his face within a foot or so of theirs, but from here on, your baby clearly knows and prefers you to anyone else in the world!

Throughout the period of three and one-half to five and one-half months, unless they are very sleepy or uncomfortable all babies seem delighted at the sight of anyone's face. Not only that, but with very few exceptions, they are very nice to look at. It is hard not to smile back at a smiling, toothless, drooling, five-and-one-half-month-old who is smiling at you. In fact, most babies of this age are irresistible.

## THE EMERGENCE OF SOCIAL AWARENESS— THE TICKLE

The beginnings of interpersonal awareness become apparent during the fifth month of life. For the first time, your baby will become ticklish.

There is plenty of evidence that a newborn can sense even a light touch. The skin or tactile receptors are far better developed at birth than their visual or auditory counterparts. What's missing during the first months of life is social awareness. For the tickle to work, a person being tickled must not only sense the touch but must also be aware that she is a "ticklee" and that somewhere nearby is a friendly "tickler." Note that normal people are incapable of tickling themselves successfully even though they are fully capable of administering and sensing a proper tickle.

The one-month-old is too immature to appreciate the required social aspect of the tickle situation. Three or four months later, however, babies reach the necessary level of social awareness.

## THE DEVELOPMENT OF
## SPECIAL SOCIAL ABILITIES

Babies cry from birth. No one has to teach them how. Contrary to what you might think, babies less than five and one-half months of age do not cry in order to get you to come to them. Rather, the cry of the newborn is simply a reflexive response to discomfort. I make this statement mainly on the basis of Piaget's studies of how the mind of a baby develops. He explains that what you see in a baby's behavior during the first few months of life is reflexive, not intentional. When you offer a three-month-old baby a rattle, he may quickly strike at it, and you may think that he "wanted" it or at least that he "wanted to hit it." Piaget demonstrated in his research that babies have no choice in the matter, that the batting of objects at three months of age is very much like the rooting (for a nipple) behavior of a newborn, along with several other abrupt mechanical actions common to all babies in the first months of life. None of the behaviors is any more "intentional" than the knee-jerk response observed when a doctor strikes the appropriate tendon.

After five and one-half months of life, it becomes increasingly obvious that babies have become capable of deliberately using the cry in order to get you to come to them. At that point, they have acquired their first social ability. The babies' new awareness marks the beginning of a wonderful and fascinating process.

## THE DEVELOPMENT OF A SOCIAL STYLE

Newborn humans can't survive on their own. If they are going to make it, at least one older, capable person must be near them from time to time to see to their needs. While they're nearly totally helpless, they do have certain assets that help guarantee their survival. One is that very help-lessness that brings out nurturing tendencies in most older human beings. The desire to nurture a baby, even if the baby is not your own, is an extremely strong human feeling that is present to some extent in most adults.

The second asset newborn babies have—it's in use from the first moments after birth—is the cry. The third important asset is the capacity to learn.

During the first months of life, learning is of a fairly simple kind called conditioning. Circumstances that happen repeatedly automatically create changes in the behavior of the human newborn, just as they do in most, if not all, other living creatures. When a three-month-old starts to suck rapidly as he sees his mother approach with a bottle or undo her bra strap, he is manifesting a typical result of the conditioning process.

## HOW A NEWBORN'S PRINCIPAL ASSETS FUNCTION TOGETHER DURING THE FIRST MONTHS OF LIFE

Very soon after birth all babies beome uncomfortable. The baby may be cold, hungry, or in pain. Whatever the source of discomfort, once it is sensed by the baby, the result is an automatic response, the cry. The cry of a newborn, particularly when it is very loud and goes on and on, is very disturbing, even at times intolerable, to adults. The effect is like that of chalk being scraped against a blackboard—only much worse. Since the baby's survival depends upon at least the occasional presence of an adult, sooner or later that person hears the crying and feels that he has to do something. Most of the time, the adult tries to make the baby feel more comfortable.

• • •

## THE THREE OUTCOMES OF
## A BABY'S DISCOMFORT

One of three things is likely to happen as a result of the adult's attempts to comfort the baby. Often the baby starts to feel better because the adult has figured out what's needed and has provided it. If you are a new mother and your baby starts to cry, you're very likely to first check his diaper. If all is well on that front (or back), you will probably look at your watch to see whether it is time for a feeding. If you have fed him recently, you may try burping him. If you are lucky, this sequence often does the trick.

The second situation, which is not at all uncommon in the first three months of a baby's life, is that you won't be able to figure out what is wrong, but you'll still be able to comfort your baby. You might offer him a pacifier or something else to suck on, such as his own fist or, in a pinch, your finger. The urge to suck, especially in the first six months of life, is remarkably strong. Though vigorous sucking obviously provides nothing but a sucking experience, the pleasure that comes from it very often stops the crying and, along with it, the baby's unhappiness.

Many parents over many years have had success rocking uncomfortable babies. At times, desperation has led others to early-morning automobile rides. Still others have tried expensive toys that generate intrauterine sounds. What all these attempts have in common is the potential to replace the discomfort the baby is feeling with some kind of harmless, distracting stimulation.

The third outcome that sometimes follows from a baby's discomfort is that you can't make the baby feel comfortable and he simply has to cry.

Regardless of the outcome, a regularity is involved in the experiences that follow an infant's discomfort during the first weeks after birth. The baby cries, and the cry is usually followed by an adult coming to the baby, talking to her, touching her, picking her up, caressing her, and so on. For most babies, that person will be her mother. From the first day of life, especially throughout the early months, and most particularly during the first ten or so weeks, this cycle of cry-response-comfort will be repeated many times every day.

While newborns' abilities to see and hear and, for that matter, to learn are quite limited, they are functional. What happens as the result of this repeated cycle is that the new infant comes to associate the various qualities of the caring adult with her feeling better. The way a mother looks, sounds, and smells are all registered over and over and over again. By the time your baby is three and one-half months of age, two interesting results can be seen in her behavior.

First of all, when the crying is not at a rage level she will at times stop as soon as she catches sight of you approaching. This new behavior, known as an "anticipatory response," is the result of the conditioning process, much like the rapid sucking that starts when the three-month-old sees his mother approaching with a bottle. The second result of these repeated early experiences is the beginnings of recognition of special people. At the Tavistock Clinic in England, researchers found that by three and one-half months or so whoever has nurtured the baby during those first weeks of life has special power in getting a child to smile more quickly and longer when compared with comparable efforts by other people. In other words, a baby will first show clear recognition of the person who has provided the bulk of the nurturing during those first weeks of life. If you haven't been with your child during those first months, whoever did around-the-clock caring for the child would be smiled at more quickly and longer than anyone else.

## CALL ME IRRESISTIBLE

Infants begin to smile from the first days of life. The amount of smiling they do during the first weeks, however, is quite limited. In fact, it seems that those first smiles don't even have much to do with sociability. Indeed, Piaget noted in his classic work on the development of intelligence that the first smiles were just as likely to be directed to a familiar toy hanging overhead as they were to the face of a parent. He made the case, which I believe is convincing, that a baby's first smiles were more a sign of familiarity than they were a sign of love or even sociability. From ten or twelve weeks on, however, there will be no mistaking the presence of your baby's smile or how often that smile is triggered by your appearance. The emergence of that absolutely wonderful behavior and the ever-increasing beauty of a child combine to make a baby more attractive than words can say, especially to his parents and grandparents.

By the middle of the fourth month, with head control almost completely developed, and with muscles and body size growing impressively, you will have an absolutely delightful person to play with. To make matters even better, toward the end of the fourth month of life most babies begin to squeal, laugh, and giggle. All in all, this is an incredibly rewarding time for parents and babies, too. You'll love it!

The remarkable attractiveness of just about all babies of this age is extremely important. Because of their long period of dependency, babies just have to have a lot of help (to put it mildly) to survive. To make sure that they get that help, they have been designed so that almost any adult who is around them regularly during the period between the fourth and seventh month falls in love with them. We use a video in our training programs of a three-and-one-half-month-old baby with a typical dynamite smile. When he breaks out into that smile to his mother, people watching the video experience a special warm feeling. The design is a success! Sadly, this friendliness toward all people by babies of this age cannot and does not continue for very long.

The huge number of comforting episodes and the increasing number of marvelous "fun times" make up a major part of a child's experiences during the first six months. When parents are able to spend a great deal of

## Birth to 5½ Months:
## Consequences of Adults' Comforting Attempts

### THE THREE SCENARIOS

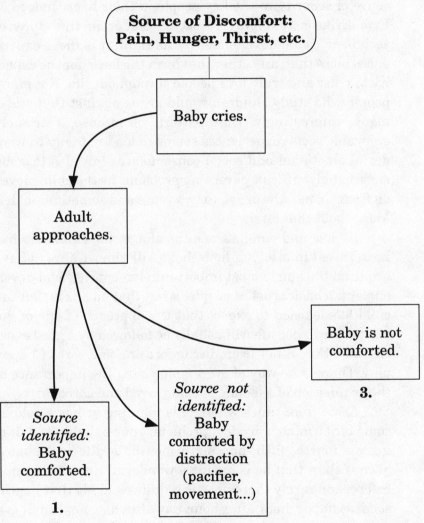

**Source of Discomfort: Pain, Hunger, Thirst, etc.**

Baby cries.

Adult approaches.

Baby is not comforted.

**3.**

*Source not identified:* Baby comforted by distraction (pacifier, movement...)

**2.**

*Source identified:* Baby comforted.

**1.**

time with their baby during the first months of life, mother, infant, and father become intertwined in an intense and exhilarating relationship. Babies drink all this in.

According to the best understanding of mental health experts, babies begin to develop a basic good feeling for and sense of security in the key people in their lives. Indeed, if Erik Erikson (a highly respected leader in the study of social-emotional development) was right, it is these experiences more than any other that form the basis for the capacity to trust and truly love people throughout life. Not many people who study children would argue against that statement. Interestingly, that pattern of intense, extremely enjoyable social experiences seems to lead not only to wonderful emotional and social consequences but also to some surprisingly difficult parenting problems as the child moves on from six months of age to two years and sometimes older. More about that later.

By five and one-half months of age, the child who has been raised in a loving household will almost always have acquired the single most important element in social development: a basic trust in people. What that means is that the child has learned to expect that the approach of one of the key people in her life will usually be followed by a good experience, either relief from discomfort or some sort of happy play. There is no way of overemphasizing the importance of the acquisition of a feeling of being loved and cared for.

Aside from times when he is teething or has a cold or some other minor physical problem, your baby's mood during his fourth, fifth, and sixth months of life will almost always show that he is having a wonderful time. At no time before, and rarely thereafter, is it quite as likely that he will seem so happy, hour after hour, day after day. For him it is a great time to simply be alive. Five-month-old babies complain only when they are uncomfortable. Their complaints are not yet directed at people. You can be sure that, if he is cranky, there is a physical reason for the distress. Your baby may be the occasional long-term colicky child or be an early teether, or he may have a painful ear infection. He may be very sleepy or hungry, but he will not be crying because he doesn't like something you have done.

Most of the time, a baby of three and one-half to five and one-half months is having a glorious time, as is that baby's parent.

## WHAT CAN GO WRONG? NOT MUCH

While it is of course true that every newborn baby is unique, they also have much in common. The same is true of parents. All babies must have a lot of help to survive. They are born with a few powerful assets—most notably the cry—and the potential to develop into one of many kinds of people. Years ago, many people thought that a child's personality was inherited. Today we have good reason to believe that parenting practices play a large role, perhaps even the major role, in the process.

Most parents share qualities that make up the core of good parenting skills. The new baby's cry draws forth feelings of tenderness and the desire to comfort. When full-blown smiling emerges during the third month of life, parents become overwhelmed with feelings of love.

As a result of these universal behaviors in babies and parents, babies receive a lot of caring, loving, and fun during the first months of life. How, then, do intelligent, loving parents get into trouble? How do well-meaning people end up with two-year-olds who are unpleasant to be with? Can you avoid such an outcome, or is it sometimes inevitable?

The first sign that social development is headed in a less than ideal direction surfaces at about seven and one-half months of age. By then some babies have developed an excessive need for attention. They complain regularly if they are not being carried or played with. Seven and one-half months is therefore a very important first checkpoint in a baby's social development.

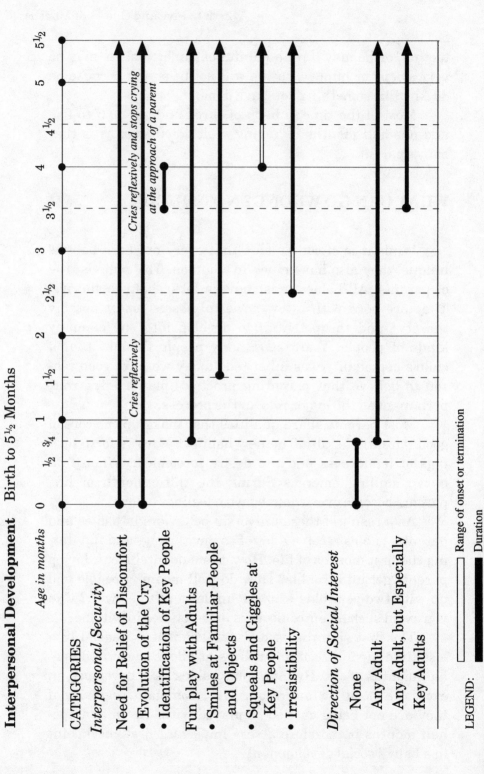

**Interpersonal Development** Birth to 5½ Months

*Age in months*

CATEGORIES

*Interpersonal Security*

Need for Relief of Discomfort
• Evolution of the Cry
• Identification of Key People

Fun play with Adults
• Smiles at Familiar People and Objects
• Squeals and Giggles at Key People
• Irresistibility

*Direction of Social Interest*

None
Any Adult
Any Adult, but Especially Key Adults

*Cries reflexively and stops crying at the approach of a parent*

*Cries reflexively*

LEGEND: ☐ Range of onset or termination
■ Duration

The second checkpoint is at fourteen months. It is truly amazing how much the typical baby has learned about her parents by then! Many a baby has already acquired a collection of bad habits, such as biting or fighting vigorously against being diapered. Most striking, however, is how some babies have become adept manipulators by this tender age. It is quite remarkable how skillfully a fourteen-month-old can use whining or screaming as a tool to get his way with his parents. Furthermore, if a baby has developed that way, it is surprisingly difficult to correct the situation. Mind you, I am talking about a fourteen-month-old!

A baby who by fourteen months regularly fights being diapered, who hits and kicks other people, and who won't take "no" for an answer inevitably gets into even deeper trouble during the balance of her second year of life. Even under the best of circumstances, such a baby will cause her parents a fair amount of grief during the fourteen-to-twenty-two-month period as she experiments with her newly sensed power in dealing with them. Socially troubled fourteen-month-olds can turn this period into a seemingly endless series of high-stress struggles. Not only is this tough on parents, but babies don't enjoy it either.

A twenty-two-month-old can be a veteran of fifteen months or so of less than ideal interactions with her parents. In that sense, a two-year-old is socially *old*. Not only is a twenty-two-month-old an "old hand" at socializing, he is also very likely to have become a powerful force in the family. It is these realities that underlie the emergence of tantrums during the third year of life. It is this kind of history of experience that leads to the "terrible twos." Also, a two- or two-and-one-half-year-old may have a baby brother or sister. Even nicely developed two-and-one-half-year-olds have a lot of trouble making room in their lives for such competition. If the older child's social development has not gone well, the situation gets to be very difficult for all concerned. But don't despair. My purpose in describing what can go wrong is only to help you avoid such pain, and I can assure you, you can.

What, if anything, could go wrong with a baby's social development during these first five and one-half months? A large body of research has led to two important conclusions: There are vital, lifelong effects that result from the experiences of the first months of life, and it is very unlikely that anything will go wrong in your case.

The most impressive body of research that addresses this question is called the maternal-deprivation studies. This work was begun during the 1940s by a psychoanalytic researcher named René Spitz. He examined the development of babies raised in orphanages who never had a chance to form a love relationship in the first few years of their lives. Until the early 1900s these children often didn't live long enough to see their second birthday! With improved health care, they survived but sadly became "psychological cripples," destined never to be able to live anything like normal lives. Subsequent studies led to a World Health Organization monograph,[*] written by John Bowlby (of England), that cited hundreds of studies of the consequences of the failure to establish an early love relationship or of the rupturing of such a relationship. The consistent central finding was that the emotional well-being of children was uniquely vulnerable during the first three years of life.

Since that time, all specialists in mental health have maintained that the first three years of life constitute a "critical period" for social and emotional development. It has become a cardinal principle for those professionally concerned with the welfare of young children that great care must be taken to see to it that every child develops and maintains a first-rate love affair during the first three years

[*]*Maternal Care and Mental Health*. Geneva: World Health Organization, Monograph 2, 1951.

of her life.* This large body of work and the total agreement of opinion, along with parallel studies of other animal species, have formed the basis for the concern that many professionals have about the extensive use of substitute care during infancy.

What that means is that during the first five and one-half months of life in particular, if you want an emotionally healthy three-year-old you have to see to it that her needs are met promptly and effectively as much of the time as possible, and you have to establish a strong, loving relationship with her.

What does all that mean for you? You have no intention of depriving your baby. The purpose of discussing maternal-deprivation research is to make clear what is at stake for your baby, emotionally and socially, during the first months of life. This issue may become very pertinent to you if you find yourself considering the use of substitute care during your baby's early months. If you do, you should be very careful. Clearly, poor-quality child care with a high infant-caregiver ratio is to be avoided at all cost.†

If you avoid using poor-quality child care, not much is likely to go wrong with respect to social development during the first five and one-half months of your baby's life.

---

*In a recent case before the state supreme court in Michigan, a direct violation of this important principle occurred. A two-and-one-half-year-old girl who had been raised by loving foster parents since she was a few days old was returned to the custody of her biological mother, who had not had any contact with her since her first week of life! The legal justification was that there had been a technical error made in the proceedings surrounding the baby's placement with the foster parents during her first week of life. This act was considered ludicrous and tragic by those of us who have studied and worked in early human development. Unfortunately, it and similar acts on the part of the justice system are common.

†A second hazard to avoid in regard to group care for very young infants is infectious disease. During the first two years of life, babies in full-time group care experience three to four times as many colds and other infectious diseases as home-reared babies.

## Neglected Babies Don't Become Spoiled

Ironically, the style of child-rearing that is required for a baby to begin to develop well emotionally is identical to the style that later leads to a spoiled child. If a new baby is allowed to cry repeatedly to no avail or to cry for long periods of time when he needs feeding, diaper changing, burping, and so on, the lesson he will learn is that crying does not pay. In orphanages, crying may not be responded to promptly, and sometimes not at all. Infants raised in such an environment cry very little once they reach six or seven months of age, and the crying they do do is caused by significant physical discomfort only. These babies do not cry to get someone's attention.

Furthermore, if people do not spend a fair amount of time enjoying the smiles and the universal beauty of a baby at three, four, and five months of age, the baby will learn that older people are not likely to be around a lot and are not likely to make life much fun. Such a child, if he survives, surely will be very unlikely to evolve into a spoiled two-year-old. Obviously, however, no one would advocate these kinds of child-rearing tactics.

## HOW TO RAISE A DELIGHTFUL CHILD

### Goals—Social Characteristics of a Delightful Three-Year-Old

What are the social qualities of a wonderful, unspoiled three-year-old?

She is happy, enjoying life most of the time rather than being a chronic complainer.

She is secure and comfortable with all people nearly all the time (except when she's ill or very tired), with only one exception. It is too much to ask of any three-year-old that she always get along well with a sibling who is within three years of her age.

She is able to share and be content with equal treatment.

She is civil and accepts her parents' authority at all times except under extraordinary circumstances (again, illness or extreme fatigue).

She is socially competent: able to get attention in a variety of socially acceptable ways; self-reliant, but able to use an adult as a resource if she can't do something for herself; justifiably proud of her achievements.

She is able to express her feelings easily. She engages frequently in make-believe behavior, especially featuring adult roles, for example, playing a doctor, a scientist, or any grown-up, in contrast to assuming the role of a baby or an animal.

She is able *both* to lead *and* to follow another child her own age.

She is aware of what a "good job" is and confident that she is capable of performing well.

I wish I could tell you that these characteristics have been studied as thoroughly as intelligence and language. They haven't. Nevertheless, my own research and the experience of outstanding preschool educators indicates that if your three-year-old meets this description, you will be living with a delightful, unspoiled child.

The first social goal for the period from birth to five and one-half months is certainly the single most important goal for parents to pursue during their child's preschool years: Each new baby must learn that she is loved passionately and unconditionally. The second goal is for the child to acquire the intentional cry for company. The third goal is for the baby to show a very keen interest in the world around her, to be bursting with curiosity. Fortunately, especially for anyone interested in a book like this, there is virtually no chance that these goals will not be achieved.

•  •  •

## COMFORTING A VERY YOUNG BABY

Though your very young infant doesn't have the mental ability to understand that you love her, your comforting efforts begin to build the love relationship from the first hours after birth. They, along with the innumerable smiling, laughing, fun experiences that increase as the weeks go by, are the means by which you demonstrate your love to your baby and at the same time begin to build her sense of security with you.

During the first ten weeks of a baby's life, you've got to expect difficulties because of the child's chronic discomfort. Occasionally parents get lucky and after the first two or three weeks their child becomes easy to care for. She may even begin to sleep for four, five or more hours at a stretch at night, in contrast to the three-hour spans you can expect during the first weeks. Easy children sleep longer and more soundly than the average. They do not seem to suffer digestive problems as often as is typical. Their parents wonder what all the fuss is about when it comes to the first months of life. (If you are blessed with an easy baby, a bit of advice: Don't talk too much about this subject to other parents with similar-aged infants.)

Unfortunately, the more common pattern is for parents to go through a stressful learning process with their babies in the first ten or so weeks. Parents get much less sleep than they're used to. They regularly feel inadequate because it usually turns out to be quite difficult to learn to comfort a normal baby during his first two and one-half months. We have found that parents usually begin to feel justifiably competent about the comforting process toward the end of the baby's third month (unless they have a colicky baby.) Soon thereafter, usually even first-time parents become more knowledgeable about how to comfort their own baby than anyone else. Here are some of the most effective tactics you should consider.

## Using a Pacifier

While some parents simply want nothing to do with pacifiers, generally those who use them have a much easier time with their baby, especially during the first six months, than those who do not. This is not to say that you will necessarily have more trouble comforting your baby if you do not use a pacifier.

Some parents try pacifiers and then announce that their baby doesn't like them. I suspect that in the majority of such cases, either the parents have ambivalent feelings about using a pacifier or they didn't know how to introduce it to their baby. Occasionally, they may be using the wrong type of pacifier. Many people expect a newborn to be able to retain a pacifier and to suck on it for several minutes at a time. In fact, during the first weeks of infancy very few babies are able to retain a pacifier for longer than a few seconds. Their tongues seem to get in the way and pop the pacifier out. This can lead to trouble, because often new parents feel they have to at least run hot water over the pacifier before they use it again. With a screaming baby in your arms, the situation easily becomes nerve-racking. There is a knack to retaining a pacifier, and unfortunately it is not an inherited knack. You have to be patient as the baby gradually acquires the ability to hang on to a pacifier. Within a month or so, most babies learn to retain one for minutes at a time.

One requirement for success is to determine, by trial and error, the type of pacifier your baby prefers. Fortunately, pacifiers are cheap. Also be sure to introduce the device without delay. The most common mistake new parents make is waiting too long before trying to get their baby to use a pacifier. Once the baby gets into a rage (which can happen quickly), she probably won't even notice that a pacifier is in her mouth. You should offer the device when the baby is uncomfortable but before she is out of control. What do you do if she gets out of control? Use the elevator move.

## The Elevator Move

This technique was developed by my wife, Janet Hodgson-White, some three years ago during our New Parents as Teachers work. Here is how to use it. Hold the baby, facing you, firmly against your upper body. Then try to duplicate the effect you experience when you are in an elevator and it stops abruptly (but not too abruptly). To do this, while holding the baby firmly against your upper body, lower yourself quickly a few inches by bending your knees. Repeat the motion many times, hesitating momentarily between knee bends.

Usually after five to ten knee bends, the baby will become less agitated and will notice the pacifier touching her lips. Ordinarily, she will clamp onto it and start to suck vigorously. Unfortunately, that may not happen the first time she quiets. Keep at it.

## Gentle Movement Through Space

Gentle movement through space has long been used to calm uncomfortable babies. Witness how many very old cradles there are. Of course, another way to provide the baby with the same experience is to hold him in your arms while using a rocking chair. You can also buy a swing (I recommend the battery-operated, motorized kind), which is usually effective between birth and about four months of age. During the baby's first three months, you will have to support both the baby's head and his torso while he is in the swing. You can obtain a support for such purposes from the same source that sells the swing, or you may do just as well with rolled-up diapers or some other kind of padding. Since swings are expensive and are only useful for perhaps twelve to fifteen weeks, I suggest you try to borrow one or find a used one.

• • •

## The Automobile Ride

It is not at all uncommon for parents to attempt to comfort an inconsolable baby by taking him for an automobile ride. Long ago, people noticed that unhappy babies frequently stopped crying and went to sleep soon after the car started moving. Many new parents take drives with their babies a few times each week between 2:00 and 5:00 A.M. A considerably more convenient alternative has recently become available. For less than $100, you can now obtain a two-part apparatus called SleepEase that produces sensations for the baby in his crib similar to those experienced during a drive! The apparatus fastens to the bottom of the crib to create the same kinds of vibrations as a moving automobile. The other element is an audiotape that produces soothing sound patterns. The accompanying literature (including research reports) seems to indicate that the system actually helps. I am not endorsing the device, just bringing it to your attention.

## Various Sound Patterns

Other means of pacifying an unhappy infant of this age involve various sound patterns. What works for some infants is the sound of a nearby vacuum cleaner. Others respond to the sound of water running from a faucet, and still others will quiet if you turn on a radio, tune it between stations so that it produces nothing but static, and then turn up the volume to the point where you can hear it across the room.

About ten years ago, one company advertised a special $50 teddy bear. Inside this stuffed animal there was a tape player that emitted sounds similar to what a fetus hears when in the womb. The rationale was that a maternal heartbeat, along with various gurgling sounds recorded from a pregnant woman's abdomen, would have a comforting effect. After all, the baby had been hearing those kinds of sounds for the better part of his life. In fact, prior to the appearance of the product, there had been a report of a study done in Japan that indicated some success using similar sounds.

I would like to bring to your attention a book on coping with a colicky baby: *Why Is My Baby Crying?* by Bruce Taubman, M.D. (New York: Fireside Books, 1990). Even though your baby may not have a serious colic condition, you may find the author's approach helpful. I've seen no evidence of research on the effectiveness of the procedures recommended in this book; nevertheless, because Taubman's recommendations make sense and are consistent with my knowledge about babies, the book might be worth reading if you're dealing with an especially uncomfortable baby. (You may not be able to find this book in a bookstore. The shelf life for most of the three dozen or so new books on babies published annually is usually less than one year. If it isn't in the bookstores, try a library.)

Most of the families my associates and I work with do quite well without either the aforementioned book or the "automobile ride" gadget, provided that they're willing to use a pacifier and to learn how to use it effectively, and provided that they're also open to experimentation with rocking devices, vacuum cleaners, running water, high-level static between radio stations, and so on, and, of course, the elevator move.

By hook or by crook, most parents become quite adept at comforting their baby by the time he is two and one-half to three months of age. The exception is the one in ten families that has to deal with a colicky baby for several additional months. They have my heartfelt sympathy; frankly, all they can do is continue to attempt to comfort the baby as best they can.

The thousands of episodes of discomfort, followed by the easing of that discomfort, usually by one or two primary caregivers, lead to the identification by the baby (at a primitive level) of her caregivers by the end of the her fourth month. The same experiences lead to the emergence during the sixth month of life of the intentional cry for company. In that sense, of course, routine comforting is the first step that ultimately makes spoiling possible. It does not, however, make it inevitable. In any event, no one who knows what babies need would recommend that you neglect an uncomfortable infant.

## SOMETIMES YOU WILL FAIL

It is very important for parents to realize that there will almost surely be times when nothing you try will work. If that happens, you have to give up and let the baby cry. Of course, you have to be certain that no illness is involved, but you should realize that babies who are not sick will at times, during their first months, become and remain very uncomfortable, regardless of your best efforts. If you refuse to accept the situation and always persist in your comforting attempts, you will wear yourself out and probably not succeed in calming your baby. If you have tried your best, if the baby is not ill, and if he is still screaming after thirty minutes or so, he may simply have to "cry it out." As heartbreaking as such episodes are, there is nothing more you can do. For most families, such events are infrequent. When such episodes are common, we say the baby is colicky.

## THE IMPACT OF COLIC

Michael was a colicky baby from the start. As was our custom, we had told his parents that by ten weeks of age, he would probably become much easier to live with. We said they could then expect a glorious, restful period from that time until he learned to crawl at about seven and one-half months. We also told them that some babies, perhaps one in eight or so, who started out particularly uncomfortable remained so well into their fourth month. We made only a passing reference to the one baby in twenty who was colicky all the way through their sixth or seventh month. Dwelling on that possibility would have been too demoralizing; after all, these folks were very tired and slightly disheartened. Unfortunately, Michael turned out to be the one in twenty! His frustrated, sleep-deprived parents tried everything. They offered Michael six kinds of pacifiers. They made frequent use of a swing, with some limited success. They carried him from room to room, for many hours every day and frequently during the night, for eight months! (Michael was a large baby and his 100-pound mother had a bad back.) They were unable to sit down to a dinner together until Michael was seven months old. Raising Michael during his first eight months was just short of one long nightmare.

The story has a happy ending. While Michael's complaining habit became unusually well developed by the time he was eight months old, his parents, with infinite patience, guided him well for the balance of his first two years. At that time Michael blossomed into a charming, happy little boy. Early colic does not inevitably lead to a cranky two-year-old.

Coping with a very young infant's bouts of discomfort, especially since they are normally very frequent during the first two months of life, is hard on parents. When you add that source of stress to the fact that you are not likely to be able to get a good night's sleep during that time, you can see why it is a good idea to get all the help you can. Mercifully, things usually get much easier as the baby enters the third month.

## HAVING FUN WITH YOUR BABY

The second major factor in helping your baby get a wonderful start is simply to have fun with her. At first she won't be very sturdy. Until she's at least three months old, her neck and back muscles won't have much strength. You can expect steady improvement, however, from the second month on. Once reliable, glorious smiling begins in the third month, you will begin to have more and more relaxed fun together. At about the same time, your baby will begin to let you catch up on your sleep and will be awake, alert, and comfortable for much longer periods during the day. You will then enter a special phase of parenting. Day by day your baby will get stronger and more responsive. By the time she is four to four and one-half months old, she will be able to hold her head erect and steady without effort, and her torso will have become sturdy. She will have begun to show a healthy zest for life. At that age, your baby will often squeal with enthusiasm and indicate that she is every bit as delighted with you as you are with her.

The huge number of fun times that you have with your baby and the equally numerous comforting experiences are inevitable. Through such natural experiences, babies and their parents fall totally in love with each other, and your baby will get off to a healthy social start in life.

## SIGNS OF THE BEGINNING OF A NEW STAGE OF DEVELOPMENT—THE EMERGENCE OF THE INTENTIONAL CRY

During the first months of life, your baby will spend a lot of time crying because she is unhappy. For any of a number of reasons she will become unhappy from time to time. She may be hungry, tired, or not feeling well, or be teething. During this period, there is no reason to think she is crying for you to come get her or to let you know she is unhappy. The picture changes, however, at about five and one-half to six months of age, when babies acquire their very first problem-solving (intelligent) ability—the intentional cry for company. This ability is a sign that your baby has had a good deal of attention and that mental development is on track. It is also the signal that the period has started when *preventable* spoiling usually beings.

CHAPTER 2

~

# Five and One-Half to
# Seven and One-Half Months

## NORMAL SOCIAL DEVELOPMENT: THE DEVELOPMENT OF INTEREST IN PEOPLE

### Early Stranger Anxiety

DURING these eight weeks or so, your baby will be very sociable and will continue to engage in lots of delightful experiences with the key people in his life. For the most part, visitors, whether family or not, will continue to receive a lovely reception. Some children, however, begin to become wary of anyone they don't live with.

Much has been written about stranger anxiety, a reality for virtually all healthy children. We used to think that it always surfaced as the child approached seven months of age and remained intense for two months or so, to be followed by a long period of shyness with strangers for the remainder of the first two years. That picture turned out to be overly simplistic.

We now now that an occasional child (one in thirty or so) shows almost no stranger anxiety at any time during the early years. Throughout the second year of life he greets everyone he meets with a big smile; if he could shake hands, he'd do that, too.

Our current view is that stranger anxiety is indeed a normal part of the social developmental process but that it varies quite a bit as to when it makes its appearance and as to its intensity and duration. That kind of variability makes teaching and parenting more complicated, but in general the following can be said with confidence.

All babies are very attractive and sociable, especially from three months on. Their attractiveness helps them obtain a deep commitment from at least one older person, something they must obtain in order to survive. That commitment is usually firmly established by the time they are seven months old. After that they begin to be concerned about whether people they do not live with represent a threat to them. When your baby approaches seven months of age, or even a few weeks earlier, you can expect a change in her behavior toward everyone other than the people she sees every day.

Instead of a quick, full smile, now her response is more likely to be a sober stare. If you are holding her in your arms, she may turn and bury her head in your upper body when someone unfamiliar approaches. That wariness may persist for five, ten, or more minutes. She may then warm up and begin to behave in a friendly way toward the stranger. An unfamiliar person who approaches rapidly, makes loud noises, and tries to pick her up may very well trigger an intense fear reaction. It makes no difference, by the way, if such a person is a grandparent.

More often than not, this shift in social style occurs at about seven months, give or take a few weeks. It can happen, however, as early as five months, or as late as nine or ten months. Stranger anxiety is less likely to happen when the baby is at home. Facial characteristics can make a difference. Some babies are particularly fearful of men with beards or women in hats. Others are fearful of men in general as compared with women, and so on.

From an evolutionary standpoint, the emergence of a fear of strangers makes sense. It indicates that the baby has identified the people he can count on for security; from this point forward, other people are to be regarded with suspicion. This period of special sensitivity to unfamiliar people usually lasts for about two months, but it may linger at a low level through most of the second year of life.

The principal social focus of your child between five and one-half and seven and one-half months of age is on the people he sees every day. Most babies throughout this age range continue to react in an endearing way to everyone, but they are more interested in their key people than in anyone else.

## THE DEVELOPMENT OF SPECIAL SOCIAL ABILITIES

### The Ability to Get Attention in Socially Acceptable Ways

Unlike the involuntary cry of the first five and one-half months, most six-month-old babies are capable of crying in order to get attention. From this point on, your baby will experiment with different kinds of cries and noises as he increases his attempts to attract the attention of the most important people in his life.

### The Intentional Cry for Company

During their first five and one-half months, babies repeatedly attract attention. They do so by simply being there and by being so precious to their parents. They do so by becoming extremely responsive and attractive as they move into the third month of life, and they do so when they make noises of one sort or another. They do not, however, cry to get your attention during the early months.

According to Piaget, the first intentional behavior an infant exhibits is moving an obstacle aside when it prevents the baby from reaching successfully for an object. He refers to this act as means-end behavior and reports that it surfaces sometime during the seventh month of life. In Piaget's view not only is this the first intentional behavior but it is also the first primitive sign of the ability to solve a problem. In that sense, it is your baby's first truly "intelligent" act.

I believe that late in the sixth month, about a month before babies begin to push obstacles aside to reach for objects, they begin to cry intentionally to attract attention. At that time, you will very probably find your baby calling for you, rather than simply crying because he is uncomfortable. The signs are easy to read: You hear your baby crying from out of sight and find, as you approach him, that he is looking in your direction, waiting for you to appear; at the sight of you he immediately stops crying and smiles. You are seeing the first signs of the intentional cry for company. A few weeks later, he will begin to hold his arms out to you, showing that he wants you to pick him up.

The emergence of the intentional cry is an excellent sign. At the same time, however, you should note that your child has entered an extraordinarily important and interesting new phase when the dimmest, slimmest sense of her impending capacity to have an effect on you has surfaced. Wait until you see where that leads you!

## The Intentional Cry and Spoon Feeding

Many parents begin to feed solid food to their babies after the first four or five months of age. Babies begin to learn important social lessons during spoon-feeding episodes, lessons that relate to the intentional cry. They begin to learn to use the cry to insist on what they want from you. Subsequent development in this area is at the core of your baby's social style.

Inevitably, when you feed your baby in a high chair, she will sooner or later show signs that she wants you to cease and desist. Either she won't want any more of what she has been accepting or you will offer her something she doesn't like. At six months, when she has acquired some skill in using her hands, she may reach out and push the spoon aside. Other behaviors could be simply firmly clenching her lips or turning her head aside. Just as surely, she will sooner or later make a noise of annoyance. All these behaviors should be expected from this age on.

Naturally, you won't insist that she continue to accept the food. If you think she's had enough or clearly doesn't like what you are offering, you will cease and desist. When that happens—and it will be a common occurrence in the weeks that follow—your child will begin to learn a basic and quite important lesson: Resisting you will sometimes stop you from doing something she doesn't want you to do. In particular, she will learn that her cries of annoyance make a difference.

It is from this very common, totally understandable type of experience that most babies begin to learn how to insist on getting their way by using a particular kind of cry, one clearly related to the cry for company but with a different starting point. In the months that follow, your baby will gradually integrate the two kinds of cries by becoming more insistent on your attention as well as becoming more adamant when she wants to resist your actions.

## WHAT TO DO WHEN THERE IS NOTHING TO DO

During the last thirty-six years—under a wide variety of circumstances, repeatedly and at great length—I've observed many children throughout the first six years of life. At most stages, babies are very interesting to watch. The nine- and ten-month-old new crawler is fascinating. The fourteen- to sixteen-month-old toddler is equally interesting.

During the first month of life babies bore me to tears. They sleep most of the time. When they are awake they tend to be either drowsy or upset about one thing or another. Once they become visually alert, at around two and one-half months of age, they begin to get interesting. They start smiling, playing with crib toys, and watching their hands. You will notice many interesting and rapid changes during the next three months. Between two and one-half and five and one-half months, almost every day brings exciting changes. Babies get stronger, better-looking, much more active, and, above all, very sociable. But development seems to slow down for a while after that.

For me, watching babies during the period between five and one-half and seven and one-half months of age was for many years a surprisingly boring enterprise. When I would go to a home to watch a six-month-old baby, she might be on the floor on a blanket, in an infant seat, or in a jump seat. Surprisingly, often that child was in her mother's arms. At six months of age, babies are almost invariably pretty to look at and generally friendly to everyone, but they don't do much of anything! On the whole, they just hang around. Every once in a while, they seem to get somewhat disgruntled and they cry, often for company. The result is that somebody may come over to them, hand them a few small toys, perhaps a rattle or two, or pick them up, carry them around, and talk to them or give them some food. All in all, it's not really much fun for an observer.

Over the last three years or so, however, we have learned quite a bit that is both interesting and of substantial importance about the period from five and one-half to seven and one-half months of age. For one thing, we have found that children need not be uninteresting to watch during this time. When they are, it is because their social development isn't being handled as well as it might.

What is the typical six-month-old baby like? She is very sociable with all people, not just her parents. She is much sturdier than she was at birth; she just exudes strength. She is likely to be chunky and have impressive arm, neck, back, and leg muscles. She has gained some control of her body. Although she cannot yet crawl across a room (about one in a hundred can, and I hope it's not yours), she can turn over both ways and balance herself in a sitting position for a few seconds. Most six-month-olds have mastered the important skill of using their hands to reach out accurately for objects to bring them close for examination, manipulation, and gumming.

She is capable of seeing clearly across a room and indeed anywhere an adult can. Her ability to hear is equally mature. We also know that all healthy six-month-olds are intensely curious about the world. She apparently is very interested in many of the objects she perceives, *but* she can't get to any of them on her own! So after playing for a while, with the few objects at hand, gumming them, transferring them from hand to hand, and throwing them, she ends up doing not much of anything at all. It seems as if there is a good deal of boredom and frustration that accompanies this lifestyle. Interestingly, and very much to the point of this book, she does have one way of alleviating that boredom and frustration, and that is through her newly acquired social tool, the cry for company.

In many homes babies start to increase the use of that cry at about six months of age. Over the next ten weeks or so, they use it more and more each day. In the process, most become increasingly insistent on being picked up and entertained. Earlier I wrote of how some one-year-old children seem to be considerably more demanding of attention than others. Well, this is why and when it starts.

• • •

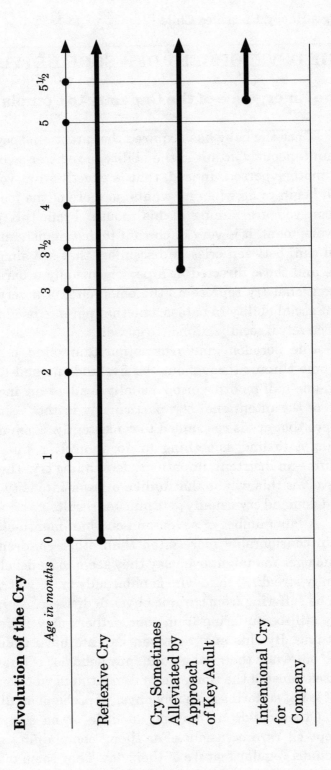

**Evolution of the Cry**

*Age in months*

Reflexive Cry

Cry Sometimes
Alleviated by
Approach
of Key Adult

Intentional Cry
for
Company

0    1    2    3    3½    4    5    5½

# THE DEVELOPMENT OF A SOCIAL STYLE

## The Emergence of the Capacity to Complain

Once the baby has acquired the intentional cry, he has simultaneously acquired the ability to register a complaint to another person. Indeed, that is exactly what your child will begin to do when he wants no more of the food in the spoon you are aiming at his mouth. From this point in development, it is very important to distinguish (as well as you can) between cries of discomfort that are aimed at no one and those directed at a person, usually a parent. The intentional cry represents the emergence of a very important social ability in babies, one that parents need to guide effectively if socialization is to go well.

The boredom and frustration that often begin and become chronic throughout the five-and-one-half-to-seven-and-one-half-month period usually lead to an increasing use of the intentional cry, particularly in those situations where that cry is responded to consistently. From a simple attempt to find something to do, it evolves into a complaint—an insistent, impatient, demanding cry. The reason it evolves this way is that unlike a lower-intensity cry, the loud demand cry usually gets quicker results.

A fair number of seven-and-one-half-month-olds complain considerably more often than other children of the same age. You might even say they seem to be developing a cranky streak. A child who is habitually cranky at this age can be suffering from chronic physical distress. A rare child may still be suffering from colic. Others may have begun teething. By this age, however, parents have usually figured out when their baby's unhappy behavior is due to such causes. Most of the time, a seven-month-old who complains a lot is not suffering from any physical problem at all.

Other children this age do little or no complaining except on rare occasions. For them, complaining has not become a regular feature of their day. They seem to be continuing to have one fine time. We have found good reasons for this disparity.

## HOW THINGS CAN GO WRONG—PAY CLOSE ATTENTION

Everyone who studies emotional development agrees that the comforting and loving care that parents provide during the first few months of life are of vital importance in building a solid emotional foundation for a baby. However, by giving the baby the care that is required for a healthy emotional start, parents simultaneously begin to build the foundation for overindulgence as well. Until your baby reaches five and one-half months of life, you have no choice but to care for her in a manner that builds both foundations. During the five-and-one-half-to-seven-and-one-half-month period, however, the situation changes. From then on, you can continue to nourish your baby's emotional needs while discouraging the development of undesirable social habits.

At the beginning of this period, intelligent, loving parents often fall into a common problem situation that is not easy to notice at first. Except when a baby is sick, teething, or uncomfortable for some other physical reason, six-month-old babies have usually developed into very attractive and precious family members. Furthermore, they are not troublesome. After all, most of them are very beautiful, and they are usually very happy to see you. This lovely state has existed for three months or so. The six-month-old baby is usually quite easy to care for, and most parents have been able to get a good night's sleep by then. But for many families, nature is about to start rocking their dreamboat.

Remember, your six-month-old can see clear across the room. (About 99 percent of all babies have nearly fully developed vision by this age.) She can now hear everything you can. Any nearby sound will cause her to turn quickly and accurately toward it. She is immensely curious about the world. She wants to get close to and explore everything she sees or hears, but on her own all she can do is sit, look, listen, smile, or fall asleep.

It is my conclusion, after watching thousands of babies throughout the first years of life, that chronic boredom and frustration very often emerge and begin to grow between five and one-half and seven and one-half months.

As my colleagues and I watch babies at home with parents, we have found that the use of the cry for company often increases steadily from five and one-half months of age on, day in and day out. Many parents may, thus, find themselves going to, picking up, and carrying their baby more and more during the sixth, seventh, and eighth months of life. A modest amount of such activity is quite pleasurable. Beyond a certain point, however, most people find it a bit tiresome. This situation very often continues until the child is at least seven and one-half months of age, at which point a new development (the ability to crawl) offers the potential for a dramatic correction.

It is at five and one-half to six months of age that "doing what comes naturally" starts to work against parents. After all, what are you supposed to do with that incredibly wonderful baby who is now likely to be wide awake far more during the day than he was in the preceding few months? He's not going to show much interest in listening to you read a book. Not many children his age watch television, even *Sesame Street*. When you give him small objects, he holds them, looks at them, and gums them, but invariably he will drop them or get tired of them. And now, though he isn't hungry or in need of a clean diaper, he cries much more frequently than he did a few weeks ago. As the days go by, the only thing that seems to keep him happy is picking him up and keeping him in your arms.

It is this situation that can and often does lead to excessive levels of crying (you could fairly call it complaining) by the time a baby is seven months old. Mercifully, however, that doesn't have to happen.

## DOING THE JOB WELL

### Goals

A seven-and-one-half-month-old who has been developing very nicely is a child who'll be very good at getting attention by making noises of one sort or another, but who will not use that tool as the dominant means to occupy himself during the course of the day.

What you should be aiming for is a child who is generally engaged in an interesting (for him) activity and who is almost always happy and rarely complains. He should show immediate interest in any new object that is offered to him. He should be very active even if he is not yet crawling. He should be practicing rolling over and pulling himself to a sitting posture, if he cannot already do so. He should enjoy any and all new activities that he is ready for (more about that subject soon). When he's sitting in a high chair he should be fascinated by the act of dropping objects off to the side. He should continue to show the zest for life that first became obvious during his fourth month.

### What to Do

Spoiling a child is not a problem during the first five and one-half months. The origins of preventable spoiling lie in the period from five and one-half to seven and one-half months. During this time, you will do well to know the details of how your baby is developing socially and to take steps to begin to guide the process effectively. The source of the difficulty lies in the common daily condition of the typical five-and-one-half-month-old baby. With increasing body strength, babies this age spend a lot of time sitting up in an infant seat or some similar device, and they soon become bored. There simply is nothing much to do. Compounding the problem is their frustration at not being able to explore all that wonderful stuff out there!

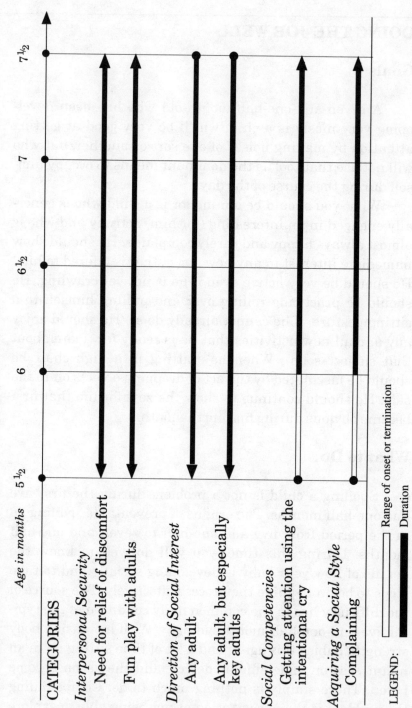

**Interpersonal Development**  5½ Months to 7½ Months

*Age in months*

CATEGORIES

*Interpersonal Security*
Need for relief of discomfort

Fun play with adults

*Direction of Social Interest*
Any adult

Any adult, but especially
key adults

*Social Competencies*
Getting attention using the
intentional cry

*Acquiring a Social Style*
Complaining

LEGEND:  Range of onset or termination

Duration

If a five-and-one-half-month-old baby could see and hear but had no interest in everything around him, there would be no problem. Five-and-one-half-month-old babies, however, are very definitely interested in investigating everything. This desire to explore becomes very obvious as soon as a baby learns to crawl across a room (at about seven and one-half months of age). It can also be seen at five and one-half months of age if you will follow these recommendations.

## The Key—Knowing What Interests a Baby and Designing a Suitable Environment

The key to helping your baby develop well socially involves understanding just what it is babies really enjoy doing at each stage. If you can learn what those interests are (and it is not all that hard to do), and if you're willing to take a few simple steps designed to make the child's daily life interesting for her, all is likely to go well during this period.

It is always sound educational practice to design a child's world in a manner that allows her to choose from several activities that strongly interest her at each stage of development. In order to learn what those rapidly changing interests are, you have to understand what is developing in a child during the first years of life.

Interests, especially during the first year, appear to be linked primarily to emerging skills. From two and one-half to five and one-half months of age, all babies show a strong interest in small nearby objects. They will handle them in a variety of ways and through such actions learn to use their hands with skill.

Five-and-one-half-month-old children are very interested in looking around at everything and anything. Using an infant seat, you can change the scenery for your child several times a day. (Remember, the infant seat at this stage of development should be placed on the floor rather than on a table because of the increasing ability of the child to tip it over.) You may, however, find it easier to use a blanket on the floor. The five-and-one-half-month old on his stomach is capable of raising the upper half of his body and looking around from that position for many minutes at a time. The baby will be interested in either watching you go about your chores or looking out a window at birds or traffic or other children or just looking at different parts of the home. Feeding the child's strong visual curiosity is part of your job as the designer of her daily activities.

Hand-eye skill development means a lot to children throughout the period from two and one-half months to two years. Now that he can handle objects with a bit more skill, if you provide a wide variety of safe, especially gummable, objects for him to handle, or bang, transfer, gum, drop, and so on, you'll be providing another element that relates well to his developmental level and his interests. I say gummable as well as suitable for handling because the sucking urge remains very strong during this time. If your baby is cutting teeth, he will be very keen on chomping down on any small, hard plastic object, such as a plastic key ring.

Unlike the crib gym, which can become a hazard as a baby learns to pull himself to a sitting position, the floor gym will continue to interest a baby throughout this period. You should give him a chance to play with it several times a day. Rather than place the baby on a blanket on the floor, it helps to place him in an infant seat in front of the toy. That way he won't have to fight gravity as he reaches to play with the object.

Babies are extremely sociable at five and one-half months, and you will have lots of fun playing together. Keep in mind that every time you *initiate* a social interchange with a five-and-one-half-month-old it's one less time that that child needs to use the cry for attention. You should therefore make a special effort during the period from five and one-half to seven and one-half months to touch base with your baby frequently. Remember, the major social goal at this time is to limit the overdevelopment of demands for attention.

You should certainly take advantage of the enjoyment that all normal babies of this age have in developing their powerful leg muscles. One of the most pleasurable activities that babies can engage in between four and one-half and nine months of age is bouncing in a seat suspended from a long spring. The original product was named the Jolly Jumper. It was well named, for most babies really do become quite jolly in these gadgets. It is one of the best toys you can buy.

At this age, babies are developing the leg muscles they will need to support themselves in a standing position, usually by the tenth or eleventh month. From the first weeks of life, the need for strong legs is anticipated in the tendency of infants to push out with their legs when they feel pressure on the soles of the feet. This behavior is known as the leg-extension reflex. As any new parent learns, a two- to three-month-old baby will repeatedly try to support her weight by pushing up with her legs when held so that her weight is partially supported on her parent's thighs. What that means for you is that as soon as your baby can have experiences that trigger that behavior, she will have another opportunity for simple enjoyment. Of course, parents can bounce children on their thighs day after day, but that gets to be a bit much.

Another reason that a baby of this age enjoys the jumper toy is her parents' responses. If you adjust the toy so that the infant's bare feet are flat on either the floor or another hard surface and are supporting a little of her weight, she will probably begin to bounce immediately. At first, she will bounce just because it feels good. But once she notices that you get a kick out of it too, she will enjoy the activity even more. This is a no-lose situation. After your child has become an enthusiastic bouncer, try playing music with a beat while she is in the jumper. You are likely to increase her fun and find her bouncing in time to the music.

It is very important to note the impact of your enthusiasm on your baby's behavior. From here on, throughout the balance of the first two years, your reactions to your baby's behaviors will be a principal factor in shaping her behaviors and, most important, *the* principal factor in shaping her social style.

Another device babies love during this period, partly because of the leg action involved, is the walker. Many physicians are dead set against walkers. The main reason is that there have been thousands of accidents involving babies in walkers—28,000 in 1991. Such a problem can't be ignored, but if a walker is used at the right age and in the right way, accidents need not occur, and the benefits can be significant in regard to social development. I recommend a walker for use only under certain conditions and for a very limited period of time (about thirteen weeks).

As with the jumper-type toy, walkers shouldn't be used before the child is four to four and one-half months of age. Younger infants don't have enough strength in their back and neck muscles to support themselves comfortably in an upright position. Once head control is mature and the child's upper torso is sturdy, both items can be used. For most normal children, that happens by the time they're four and one-half to five months of age.

I strongly recommend up to fifteen minutes at a time, up to four times a day, for both the jumper and the walker. A baby in either situation is not a bored, frustrated baby. In the case of the bouncer, babies have a wonderful time from the start. It is an absolutely wonderful gadget. We have checked with leading pediatric orthopedists. It is their opinion that as long as the baby is physically normal, there is nothing wrong with using such a device.

The walker is even better. It not only facilitates activity of the large leg muscles, it also allows a baby to explore. Of course, an exploring baby moving around a house is generally a baby in danger. That is why we strongly insist that *if you use a walker at any age, you do so only when you can be there to watch every single moment.* If you do watch whenever your child is in a walker, you don't have to worry that she might fall off the top of a flight of stairs. You will find that your baby will begin to teach you how to safety-proof your home; he will find things that are worrisome that you might not have noticed—a dangling cord, a piece of a plant that is hanging within reach, and so forth.

If you use the jumper or the walker, be careful about the distance between the baby's behind and the floor, and be sure the baby's feet are bare.[*] For the distance to the floor to be correct, the baby should not be on tiptoes, nor should her legs be bent too much. Picture the position of a skier, with both feet firmly planted, but with the knees bent only partially.

Walkers often come equipped with an overhanging bar from which several small objects dangle in front of the baby. The objects are supposed to keep the baby occupied, but the major reason walkers can be so much fun for babies of this age is that the device allows the baby to get to all those enticing objects and places that he wants to explore up close. Having small objects hanging a few inches away has nothing to do with the baby's desire to get out and see the world. They simply obstruct the view. Furthermore, such objects are not very appealing to babies anyway. The bar, with objects attached, can be removed with hardly any effort. I suggest you take it off.

---

[*]I urge you not to put anything on your baby's feet when she is at home, throughout the first two years of life. Not only will she have much more fun in a jumper or a walker; more importantly, she won't have to cope with yet another obstacle. Shoes, sneakers, and socks, even those with gripping pads, all make physical activity more difficult for infants. Just as you pay strict attention to colds and earaches to make sure your baby can hear well throughout the early years, you should help her in her innumerable attempts at mastering and enjoying her body. For these purposes, nothing beats bare feet. Naturally, you may worry about her feet getting cold, particularly when it is cold outside. Consult your pediatrician if you are concerned about this issue. We have never encountered medical opposition to our recommendation.

If you follow these directions, your baby will be enjoying the jumper after a very short time, if not immediately. If you see any indications of displeasure, remove the baby promptly and try the activity the next day.

When babies are put into a walker for the first time, most just sit there. A few will quickly push their legs against the floor and move, but in nearly all such cases they move backward. It usually takes several days for the baby to acquire the next level of skill, moving sideways. After two weeks or so, babies begin to lean forward and move ahead as well. From then on, there is no stopping them. Most babies show increasing delight in using the walker day by day. Young infants find the walker easiest to use on hard, smooth surfaces such as tile or wood flooring. High-pile carpets are often too difficult to cope with. High thresholds are also a problem. As they get bigger, stronger, and more skillful, however, not much in the average home will stop or slow down a determined baby in a walker.

**IMPORTANT:** Use a walker only when you can pay full attention. When your baby acquires the ability to make it across the room on his own (by crawling or even rolling), stop using it! There is no reason for its continued use.

Once again, use the gadget only when you can watch, and don't use it or the jumper for more than one hour each per day. Limiting the time in these devices is important because babies need to spend time on a flat surface (like the floor) in order to practice mastery of the body. The five-and-one-half-month-old, for example, is practicing turning over and will soon be practicing pulling up to a sitting posture. She needs a lot of practice to master such skills.

Remember, a not yet crawling baby in a walker is in more danger than such a baby on the floor on a blanket. Even if you are watching him every minute, that's really not enough. You should also closely examine your home for possible dangers. A baby in a walker may be able get her fingers squeezed in a doorjamb or pull on the cord from an iron. If you don't stay reasonably close to the child once he becomes able to move quickly in the walker, he may get to one of those hazards before you can. He may also move quickly to a swinging door or squeeze a finger in a drawer.

You may decide that using a walker isn't worth going through what I have just described. Parents who have made use of a walker the way I have recommended have invariably been delighted with the results. You won't regret it.

## How to Handle Sleep Situations

Generally, barring painful teething, middle-ear problems, or other physical ailments, babies in this age range settle into a regular, easy-to-live-with sleep pattern. Sleep problems may take root at this time, however, so preventive tactics are desirable.

First of all, deciding that a baby should take a nap or be put to sleep for the night on the basis of what time it is can get you into significant trouble. It is far wiser to be guided by sleep signs rather than by your watch. Five-and-one-half-month-old babies do not attempt to hide the fact that they are sleepy. They yawn, rub their eyes, open and close their eyes, and get cranky. My advice is: Be on the watch for sleep signs when an infant of this age has been awake for three hours or so. Do *not* immediately pick up the baby and put him in the crib. Instead, wait until you see signs of exhaustion. It usually doesn't take long, rarely more than an additional fifteen minutes or so. The longer you wait, the fewer sleep problems you are likely to have.

If, after you have seen the signs of exhaustion and put the baby down, he begins to cry, do *not* quickly pick him up. Leave the room. Close the door. Note the time. Give it five minutes. Chances are very good that he will fall asleep during that time. Notice that I said chances are very good. During these early months, two kinds of factors can intrude at this point. The baby may be uncomfortable because of a physical problem—for example, an earache or teething—or you may be dealing with a false alarm. If you don't believe the baby is ill and he is still crying after five minutes, I suggest you take him out of the crib, give him something to do, and begin again to watch for sleep signs. They will probably reappear soon. When they do, repeat the procedures.

In the case of illness, this routine is obviously not suitable. You should do everything you can to make the baby as comfortable as possible. Remember, sometimes nothing will work and he will just have to cry it out. Let's hope that such episodes are rare.

Some parents establish various routines around nap or sleep time. Breastfeeding mothers often offer the breast in the hope that the baby will fall asleep while nursing. Others try to rock the baby to sleep in their arms. Others use music or even a bedtime story. From what we have seen fairly often in our work with families, most of these routines tend to interfere with rather than facilitate the process. Some children treated with such routines at this stage of development seem to acquire a demand for them. In such cases parents may find that demand increasing and the process of getting the baby to sleep becoming quite lengthy.

Toward the end of the second year of life, children become mature enough to truly appreciate stories. From then on, bedtime stories usually become very enjoyable and helpful. Between five and one-half and seven and one-half months, however, I believe the best approach is to keep the sleep situation simple. When your baby is sleepy, she will go to sleep. Indeed, you won't be able to keep her awake.

From this point in a baby's life on through the second birthday, sleep is a classic site for socialization problems. Many an eighteen-month-old child who has been overly catered to makes nighttime a chronic horror for his parents. Parents of such children often find themselves exhausted. Some have told us they simply couldn't take it anymore. My wife has a simple song she recommends parents sing to the baby who wants to get out of his crib at three in the morning: "Nighttime is bedtime. Bedtime is sleeptime. I love you. Goodnight" (to be sung in a sprightly manner).

## SUMMARY

Spoiling usually gets its start during the period from five and one-half to seven and one-half months. It is rooted in the very common possibility of a baby becoming bored and frustrated during this period, which begins at around five months of age, when he becomes comfortable sitting up (with support). It lasts until he acquires the ability to crawl about the home. The one thing babies can do to alleviate the boredom and frustration is to use their new social tool, the cry, in order to get an adult to come to them. If, day after day, there is nothing much else to do, they will steadily increase its use.

The key to holding down the excessive development of this kind of crying is to provide interesting things for the baby to do. Identifying what might be interesting is easiest when you learn what babies of this age really enjoy and what they are capable of. If you will feed your baby's visual and hand-eye interest, his need to chew on hard objects, and his enjoyment of socializing with you, along with his pleasure in vigorous leg exercise and exploration, your child will move through the period of five and one-half to seven and one-half months having a great time. You won't have to lug around an increasingly heavy child because he will usually be busy having a great time.

Make a special effort during the period from five and one-half to seven and one-half months to go to the baby *before* she cries for you to play with her. By doing so you will be helping to prevent overdevelopment of the intentional cry for company. The more you engage in that kind of behavior, the less likely she will be to demand more and more of your attention each day.

Emancipation, however, is coming soon. Once the child achieves the ability to move across a room on her own, you will no longer have to worry about boredom, unless you choose to prevent or severely restrict her activity. That doesn't mean you'll have nothing to worry about, but what you'll have to pay attention to will shift from the baby's boredom and frustration to other issues, all of which you will be able to deal with.

## SIGNS THAT A NEW STAGE IS BEGINNING: THE EMERGENCE OF THE ABILITY TO GET ACROSS A ROOM ON HIS OWN

All sorts of remarkable new developments begin at about seven and one-half months of age. The most conspicuous is the ability of a baby to get around on his own. The result is a dramatic change in daily life (provided that the big people who control things allow the baby to explore rather than plop him in a playpen).

While his new ability to crawl across a room is the most obvious new development, the changes that begin in the social realm are even more exciting and numerous. In the next chapter, I will discuss the emergence of very important social abilities and the details of three critical social lessons that babies deal with during the period from seven and one-half to fourteen months of life.

~

# CHAPTER 3

# Seven and One-Half to Fourteen Months

"You're not going to send me up there all alone, are you?"

*—Incredulous response from the father of ten-month-old twins to his wife's request that he go to the nursery and change the babies' diapers*

## NORMAL SOCIAL DEVELOPMENT

WHAT happens in the life of a child between seven and one-half and twenty-four months of age is of critical importance in the shaping of a person. If you have an absolutely delightful and secure two-year-old child who is comfortable and effective in interchanges with family and other adults, you will have a three-year-old who is even more wonderful socially. Indeed, I believe that child will be successful in these respects all the way through the first decade of life and perhaps even beyond. I wish I could prove that statement, but I can't. Nobody has done the research that's required to either prove or disprove such a claim. Nevertheless, I'm convinced of the validity of these statements, which are based on my observations over a long period of time.

## NATURE VERSUS NURTURE

Many students of human development have empha-
sized the qualities babies are born with and their contribution to the child's growing personality. I certainly can't deny
some important role for factors such as energy or activity
level, quickness, age at the onset of crawling and walking—
all qualities that come with the child and are not easily modified. But whether a child is impatient with restrictions, or
kind, or nasty, or selfish, or caring—these basic characteristics that make up the majority of a three-year-old child's
social style seem to me to be shaped by the adults in his
environment during the formative period between seven
and one-half and twenty-four months of age. I simply do not
agree with those who claim that the "difficult" child was
genetically destined to develop into an unbearable two-and-
one-half-year-old. I might add that there is absolutely no
research to support such a position.

## THE DEVELOPMENT OF
## INTEREST IN PEOPLE

### Stranger Anxiety

From seven and one-half to fourteen months, the wariness toward strangers exhibited in the preceding weeks
intensifies. The message seems to be "I need my key people,
especially when I'm not at home. As for all those others, I
just don't know; they may not be friends. Before I relax with
them, I'd better check them out."

During this period, your baby's social life will be very
narrowly focused on the people she lives with. From this
point on, your baby will studiously accumulate knowledge
about your responses to her during feeding, diapering, bath
time, indeed any time you interact. She will, of course, pur-

sue the satisfaction of her curiosity and the mastery of her body, but those interests will certainly be no more important to her than the social lessons she learns as she interacts with the key people in her life.

At this stage of life, peers are of no more interest to her than squirrels or birds. The same is true for younger infants. A ten-month-old may look for a few moments at a younger infant but won't show any sustained curiosity.

## Separation Anxiety

Closely related to the expected stranger anxiety of this period is the appearance of separation anxiety. The most common sign of this new phase is when your nine-, ten-, or eleven-month-old cries as his mother begins to leave the room. In the more dramatic form of separation anxiety, a baby may cry bitterly when a mother attempts to make the departure less distressing by handing him to his father. The baby's unhappiness at this prospect often hurts his father's feelings. However, such behavior has to be expected and endured. Research has shown that babies of this age who have been raised in orphanages where no single person has spent a great deal of time with them at any age will allow anyone to hold them and will not complain when they are left. Such a baby has failed to form an attachment to anyone, and his prospects for a healthy adult life are very slim. So fathers, instead of feeling hurt, you should regard your son's preference for his mother as a healthy sign. Of course, if you are his primary caregiver, he may cling to you when you try to hand him to his mother!

Separation anxiety is generally most intense in the last months of the first year, but it can persist for several months into the second year. Like so much else in human development, if it goes on and on it will become a symptom of less than ideal development.

• • •

## Sibling Rivalry

To ignore the impact of sibling rivalry on the evolution of social development would be most unwise. It is during this period of seven and one-half to fourteen months, when a baby becomes mobile, that you can expect sibling rivalry to develop if there is a slightly older sibling in the home, particularly a first child who is less than three years older than the baby. I've discussed this subject at great length in *The First Three Years of Life** and introduce it here because close spacing of children makes a huge impact on the direction of the seven-and-one-half- to fourteen-month-old baby's interest in people. The direction of social interest of a first child is almost exclusively toward her parents at this age. A closely spaced younger sibling has no such luxury.

The normal, increasingly frequent episodes of jealousy and aggression initiated at this stage by the older child naturally play an important role in the socialization process. The younger baby in this situation learns something about hostility and about how to defend himself that a first child ordinarily does not. Precisely what the consequences of this early learning are no one really knows, but on a day-to-day basis parents need to be aware of the inevitability of these episodes and know how to minimize their negative effects.

Instead of concentrating all his social learning on the key adults in his life, the baby with a closely spaced older sibling is forced into learning about her as well. While, in general, social lessons learned about an older sister are nowhere near as important as those learned about his parents, when it comes to self-defense the baby will pay attention. This awareness is illustrated by the many one-year-old babies who will flinch and cry as soon as an older sibling approaches.

In addition to self-defense lessons, there certainly will

*See especially pps. 246–48.

be loving moments between closely spaced siblings, but don't expect them to be as numerous as episodes of jealousy.

## THE DEVELOPMENT OF SPECIAL SOCIAL ABILITIES

The period from seven and one-half to fourteen months is the time in life when the following social abilities of major significance emerge.

Babies begin to use an adult as a resource when they determine they can't do something for themselves.

Babies begin to express their feelings, both affection and annoyance, to an adult.

Babies begin to show pride in their achievements.

Babies begin to engage in pretend or make-believe play.

These four abilities, along with an effective style of getting attention, are characteristics that indicate especially fine social development during the first years of life. They are a major part of what is special about the social behavior of beautifully developed three- to six-year-old children.

During this brief period of early life, from seven and one-half to fourteen months, these attributes begin to surface. I am convinced that whether these important behaviors develop well or not depends directly on how adults respond to them during a baby's first three years of life. This conviction of mine is a major reason why I urge you to do everything you can to see to it that your baby spends the majority of her waking hours with you and her grandparents during her first three years. While there are of course exceptions, on the whole I believe those six people are more likely to nourish the best development of these social qualities than anyone else.

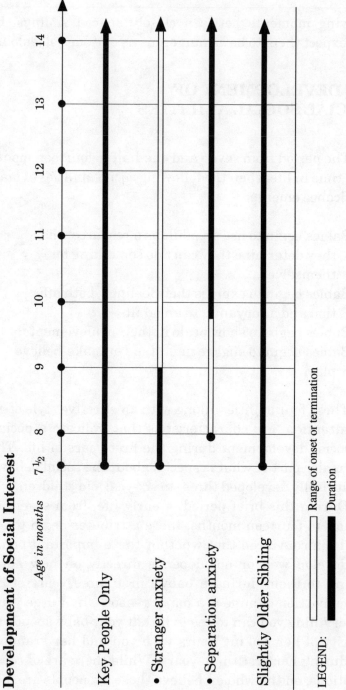

Development of Social Interest

*Age in months*

Key People Only

• Stranger anxiety

• Separation anxiety

Slightly Older Sibling

LEGEND:
☐ Range of onset or termination
■ Duration

7½  8  9  10  11  12  13  14

## Using an Adult as a Resource

You will see this delightful sign of progress when your baby is between nine and one-half and eleven months of age. It will be clear that he is not simply asking for attention (which is much more common at first) but that he wants help with a particular goal, such as more juice or more crackers. Since his ability to use words is still far too limited, he will make his wishes known with a gesture or a sound.

## Expressing Feelings, Both Positive and Negative, Toward an Adult

Sometime between nine and one-half and eleven months of age, your baby will very probably begin to hug or kiss you without being asked. At about the same age, perhaps a few weeks later, she will begin to express anger at you at suitable times. Although babies become angry and express rage from the first days of life, they express anger toward another person only from about eleven months on. The distinction is that when a four-month-old is in a rage he is not likely to be looking you in the eye, nor has his expression of anger immediately followed a behavior on your part. But the nine-and-one-half- to eleven-month-old will express anger at *you* when you try to get him to do something he doesn't want to do (for example, hold still to be diapered) or when you try to prevent him from doing something he wants to do (play with the dog's food). At first you may not be sure that he is really directing his anger at you, but rest assured, in a few weeks you will be.

## Showing Pride in Achievement

The achievement of the ability to sit up on her own, pull to stand, get down safely, cruise, walk—all happen (for about three-quarters of all children) between seven and one-half and twelve months of age. Each one of these land-mark achievements requires lots of practice and lots of effort. Each success provides an opportunity for enthusias-tic praise from grown-ups. By ten and one-half or eleven months of age, the typical baby, who now has had a good deal of such experience, makes it quite clear that she knows that she is praiseworthy. Immediately after completing a difficult or cute act, your ten- or eleven-month-old baby is very likely to turn toward you with a great big smile on her face. At this point, she may also give herself a hand in recognition of her accomplishment.

At times, when I have appeared on television, families with their two-year-old children have been on stage with me. At breaks for commercials, the studio audience will abruptly applaud at the urging of the studio workers. Most two-year-olds respond the same way in such situations. As soon as they hear the applause, they turn toward the audi-ence and glow, basking in the adulation. There is apparent-ly no doubt in their minds about who the applause is for. Why should there be?

## Engaging in Make-Believe or Pretend Play

This kind of behavior usually surfaces shortly after the first birthday, usually before fourteen months. Its first form often involves the telephone and make-believe conversa-tions. (Most babies prefer real telephones to toy ones.) Shortly thereafter, you're likely to see your baby imitating household chores he has observed you doing. Remember, imitation begins to be a major factor in a child's behavior during the last few months of the first year. The tendency to imitate adult behavior and to mimic words becomes very strong during the second year of life.

• • •

# THE DEVELOPMENT OF A SOCIAL STYLE

## Three Critical Social Lessons

During the period of life from seven and one-half to fourteen months, all children face three critical social lessons: learning about the effects of varying degrees of crying; acquiring good and bad habits; and learning to insist on getting one's own way.

### LEARNING ABOUT THE EFFECTS OF VARYING DEGREES OF CRYING

Between seven and one-half and eleven and one-half months of age, most children go through a basic sequence of achievements in respect to the control of their bodies. I'm referring mostly to large-muscle skills rather than hand-eye ability which also undergoes steady improvement during this time period. The seven-and-one-half-month-old child has usually just achieved two very important large-muscle abilities.*

He can get to a sitting position on his own. That's pretty impressive, but nowhere near as consequential as the other motor achievement that happens at about the same time, the ability to move across a room on his own. From then on, life changes dramatically for all parties. Crawling is the most common first form of locomotion, but some babies will scoot, and a few will use their recently acquired ability to turn over to roll from place to place! Clearly, the urge to explore is very powerful in the typical seven-and-one-half-month-old infant.

*When I say these abilities have just been achieved, I'm talking about approximately three-quarters of all children, of whom a small percentage have achieved these abilities weeks and occasionally even a couple of months earlier than this date, while other normal babies may not master these skills for another few months. For more detail on this subject, see *The First Three Years of Life,* especially the charts describing motor development.

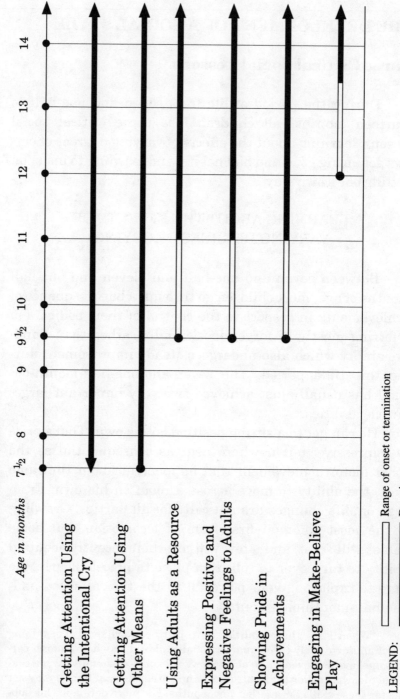

# Development of Social Competencies

**Age in months**

| | 7½ | 8 | 9 | 9½ | 10 | 11 | 12 | 13 | 14 |
|---|---|---|---|---|---|---|---|---|---|

Getting Attention Using
the Intentional Cry

Getting Attention Using
Other Means

Using Adults as a Resource

Expressing Positive and
Negative Feelings to Adults

Showing Pride in
Achievements

Engaging in Make-Believe
Play

LEGEND:     Range of onset or termination

            Duration

At seven and one-half months, about three-quarters of all babies are able to crawl across a room. Like a kitten or a puppy that's just become mobile, they will investigate anything they can get close to, given the chance. They seem to be consumed by curiosity. Human beings have fewer instinctive behaviors to help them cope with the world but a far greater capacity for learning than any other animal creature. Because of this reality, pure curiosity has long been held to be a particularly important quality in babies.

By nine months of age, the first climbing ability usually surfaces; it consists principally of the ability to climb heights of a maximum of eight or nine inches. This new skill is enough to allow a baby to climb *up* most stairs. Unfortunately, the ability to climb *up* stairs is not accompanied by the ability to climb *down* stairs. Over the next two months, you can teach your baby to climb down stairs on his stomach. You can use a low bed or sofa to show him how to turn around so that his feet face the edge of the bed; then he can gently lower himself to the floor. With a little help, he will transfer that action to the stairs.

At about ten to ten and one-half months of age, the next talent surfaces: the ability to pull himself to a standing position by using a prop of some sort to lean on. This prop is more often than not furniture, but it can be a human leg or a floor lamp. The ability to pull to stand requires that he deal rather quickly with the problem of getting back down to the floor without hurting himself. Practice begins immediately, and it generally doesn't take too long (a few days to a week) before the baby can prevent damage to himself in these situations.

Ben and Sam (twins) both began to pull to stand at about eleven months of age. Their parents were typically loving and attentive, perhaps somewhat extra-attentive because the boys were born a few weeks early. Once they became able to, both pulled to stand frequently. Neither, however, made any attempt to learn on his own to get down. Instead, every time they pulled to stand they cried for someone to help them down. Day by day, this behavior became more frequent as they inevitably started to pull to stand on coffee tables and their floor gym.

Their mother was an unusually bright, well-educated, and fun person. She couldn't figure out what to do! She was running to the boys dozens of times every day. In the process, the boys were clearly beginning to acquire a habit of crying insistently for help.

I was surprised at the situation, which doesn't happen very often. What is much more common is that babies teach themselves how to get down from a standing position a few days after they first learn to pull to stand. I explained to her that as with going down stairs, she could teach the boys how to get down from a standing position to the floor. If she showed them how to bend their legs and lower one arm to the floor, they would get the hang of it within a few days. In any event, I pointed out that sooner or later they were going to have to learn to get down by themselves. That made sense to her, but the boys seemed so scared! She wasn't confident that after showing them what to do, she could sit by and watch them without helping. Nor was she at all confident that they would try to get down on their own within a matter of days.

I coached her through the procedure with one of the boys, and then I left. The next morning she called, brimming with gratitude and wonder. Both boys had already mastered the skill!

The same sort of disbelief is common among first-time parents when it comes to teaching their babies to climb down stairs. I have met many parents of fourteen-month-old children who just can't believe that their child will learn to climb safely down stairs on his stomach at that age, though, in fact, very few babies cannot learn to do so by one year of age.

At about ten and one-half months of age, your routinely standing infant will begin to "cruise," an activity in which he moves about while holding on for support to a coffee table or the edge of a chair. Between eleven and eleven and one-half months, he can be taught to come downstairs backward on his stomach. Also at about this age, most children take their first unassisted steps. By then, climbing ability has progressed to the point where they usually can climb sofas, sofa arms, sofa backs, and kitchen chairs.

This *sequence* is usually invariable, although of course the *age* of each achievement, like that of many developments in the first years of life, varies rather broadly. You need not worry even if your baby doesn't take her first steps until she is eighteen months old. Such late walking usually has no significance at all for later development.

This series of achievements of control over the body is always difficult for infants. It requires a great deal of practice and very often results in minor accidents. Your baby, as he learns to sit by himself, may very well lose his balance and topple over, sometimes backward, and he may hit the back of his head on the floor. That can really hurt! The pain, while real, is usually quite short-lived, lasting no more than a minute or two. There are, however, exceptions. Some pain caused this way can last several minutes, but such an episode rarely leads to any significant damage.

Not only will your baby's balance be poor during this four-month period, but so too is his judgment and his ability to correct an error rapidly. When he is learning to pull himself up to a standing position, he may occasionally reach for something to grab, miss it, and bump his head, or he may squeeze a finger in a drawer or a doorjamb. All roaming babies suffer such minor accidents frequently during the seven-and-one-half to eleven-and-one-half month period of life, a period when your baby's forehead will usually feature one or two black-and-blue marks most days.

Occasionally, your baby may fall and cry—out of a combination of surprise and fear, rather than pain. In those instances when pain is the cause, her cry may last a bit longer, and obviously you should do everything you can to comfort her. When a baby squeezes her finger or bumps her head, she will feel pain and cry. The person caring for the baby usually hears the cry and responds. Styles of response by adults generally fall into two categories.

In the first category, all cries are responded to immediately. If the crying seems to indicate the baby is feeling more than a very minor amount of discomfort, the adult quickly drops what she is doing, goes to the baby, picks her up, and tries to comfort her in any way possible. Such comforting generally takes no more than a couple of minutes. The baby is then turned loose to continue her explorations. When the baby's cries don't have an urgent quality, the adult still responds promptly, but without rushing to the child and picking her up for comforting. Instead, the adult says something that is intended to comfort the baby from a distance and waits a moment or two to see if the baby is okay. If the child continues to cry, the adult goes to the baby and tries to comfort and distract her. If that doesn't work, she will pick the child up and try even harder to make her comfortable.

In the second child-rearing style, every time the baby cries, regardless of whether it is a loud or soft cry, the adult drops whatever she is doing and moves quickly to pick him up and comfort him. As you might imagine, this pattern is repeated many times every day. Adults who behave this way seem excessively nervous and, of course, overprotective. I can't help feeling that for them, child-rearing is much less enjoyable than it is for others.

These two styles of parenting, both common, lead to different uses of the cry in one-year-old children. Parents who respond quickly to a baby's every cry by picking him up and attempting to console him, regardless of whether the pain is substantial or not, find themselves living with a "crybaby" by the time he is one year of age. Such babies, sadly, are quicker to cry, and they do so far more than most one-year-olds. Such babies have clearly been taught to behave that way during their preceding five months of life, and they get into the habit of complaining frequently every day. I can assure you that this is no fun for anyone, including the child. On the other hand, babies whose parents respond to minor mishaps by offering verbal reassurance, and occasionally distraction, learn, during the seven-and-one-half to fourteen-month period, to take minor misfortunes in stride.

## ACQUIRING HABITS—GOOD AND BAD

During their first seven and one-half months, all healthy children become increasingly curious about the world. But once a baby begins to be able to move her body forward, even if only a few inches, curiosity shifts into high gear. At this stage, babies will wear themselves out dragging themselves with their forearms, if necessary, to get to whatever interests them. Once they become able to crawl across a room, they will regularly show every bit as much curiosity as a kitten does. One particularly striking example is always seen in the area of hand-eye activities.

Remember, your baby has learned to use her hands to reach for objects only during the sixth month of life. Acquiring additional hand-eye skills is a consuming interest of normal babies during the balance of the first two years of life. Seven-and-one-half- to eleven-month-old children will become enthralled by the results of turning a light on in a dim room or flushing a toilet or pushing the power switch on an instant-on television or radio. Most children want to perform these acts repeatedly during the last months preceding their first birthday. Pity the poor parents who have a nice television set that cannot easily be screened off from the now mobile ten-and-one-half-month-old child. She will crawl over to the set, pull to stand, and push the on/off button over and over and over again, watching with delight for the appearance of the picture and listening for the sound that follows immediately upon the simple act of pushing the little button. However, babies don't need anything quite as dramatic as television action. We've watched babies engage

# 7½ to 14 Months:
# Taking Small Mishaps in Stride

## PARENTING STYLES
*1. Overreactive Style*

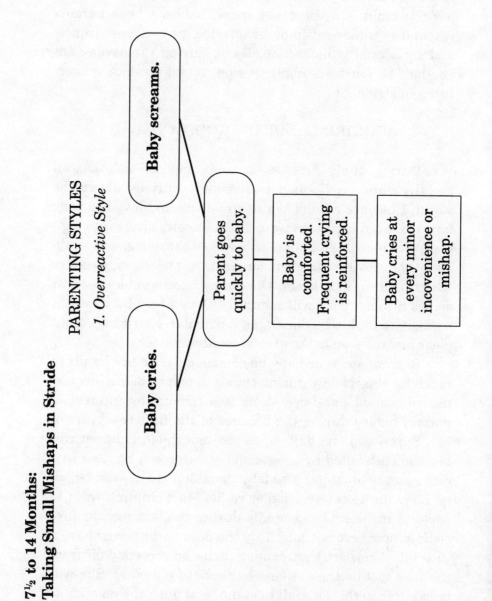

Baby cries.

Baby screams.

Parent goes quickly to baby.

Baby is comforted. Frequent crying is reinforced.

Baby cries at every minor incovenience or mishap.

## 2. Optimal Style

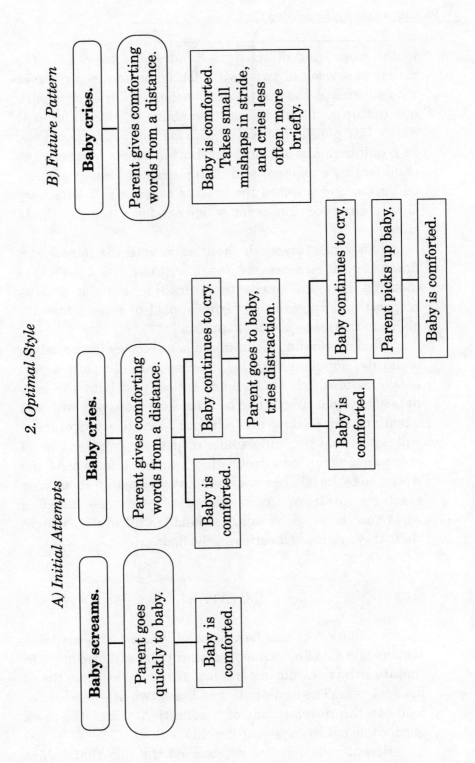

A) Initial Attempts

**Baby screams.**
Parent goes quickly to baby.
Baby is comforted.

**Baby cries.**
Parent gives comforting words from a distance.
Baby is comforted.

Baby continues to cry.
Parent goes to baby, tries distraction.
Baby is comforted.

Baby continues to cry.
Parent picks up baby.
Baby is comforted.

B) Future Pattern

**Baby cries.**
Parent gives comforting words from a distance.
Baby is comforted. Takes small mishaps in stride, and cries less often, more briefly.

in the same kind of activity—hundreds of times over the course of a week or two—with double-button energy-saver mechanisms on the front of dishwashers. All they do is push one button and wait to hear the sharp "click" sound as it moves into place. They watch with fascination as it depresses a half inch and the adjacent button comes forward. The child pauses a moment and then pushes the newly projected button and watches the process repeat itself. This very simple situation has a lot of appeal for a ten-month-old child.

This almost hypnotic fascination with the immediate, dramatic consequences of newly acquired hand-eye skills (nothing is more potent than flushing a toilet in this respect) underlies the powerful appeal of pop-up toys for eight- to fourteen-month-old babies.

This newfound fascination also coincides in the baby's social development with his keen examination of his parents' reactions to his behaviors. At first your baby will take note of how you react when he refuses to cooperate with you when you are feeding him with a spoon. In particular, he will notice that you will usually respect his small sounds of annoyance when he rejects what you are offering. As the weeks go by, he will become quite knowledgeable about your reactions to all aspects of such eating scenes—including what you do when he smears bananas all over his high-chair tray or drops Cheerios on the floor.

## IMITATION

In addition to this new focus of interest on your reactions to certain of his behaviors, your baby will also begin to imitate behaviors during the last three or four months of his first year. The combination of these two new tendencies leads to the development of a collection of habits—some good, some not so good—during this period.

Recent research has established the fact that babies

can, in a very limited way, imitate what they see even as early as the first few weeks of life. If an adult faces a baby less than a month old and sticks out his tongue, the baby may then attempt the same sort of behavior in response. Because the report of such unexpected behavior has been confirmed by other studies, some students of human development have claimed that imitation starts at a few weeks of age and from then on is a regular feature of the baby's behavior. Clearly, this is not the case, because the only confirmed type of early imitative behavior, tongue protrusion, disappears by the second month of life. Subsequently, babies show no other genuine imitation until the last three to four months of their first year. From then on, imitation grows steadily, becoming very frequent during the second half of the second year of life.

Babies will begin to respond when they're encouraged to play patty-cake, play peek-a-boo, or wave bye-bye during the last few months of their first year. They certainly will not behave this way when they're five or six months of age. One reason patty-cake and peek-a-boo come into an infant's repertoire between ten and eleven months of age is the simple tendency to imitate. The remarkable reinforcing power of typical parental responses to the baby's first successes with these games is another reason.

If you start to play peek-a-boo with your nine- or ten-month-old, she will pay attention and sooner or later will, in her own simple way, attempt something like it. You will get a huge kick out of her version of peek-a-boo and probably immediately show a lot of enthusiasm. Your baby will pay very close attention to your behavior as part of her ongoing study of her effects on you. Increasingly, when you start a peek-a-boo game, she will imitate you and look for your enthusiastic response. Your immediate, unusual, and mildly explosive response reinforces her behavior, as the days go by, she will become more and more reliable at peek-a-boo, patty-cake, and waving bye-bye.

This reinforcement is also true in the case of funny

faces and actions like bending down and looking backward through her legs or turning around and around until she gets dizzy. Twelve- to fourteen-month-old children very often have a repertoire of funny faces that they delight in using. They obviously expect that when they make these faces to adults, their parents and others as well, there will be a dramatic, approving response. That is precisely why they do it.

Unfortunately, this period from eight months on through to eleven months usually sees the emergence of unpleasant habits as well. The list is fairly long. Biting a nipple, a shoulder, or a face; pulling hair, earrings (especially Mom's pierced ears), or necklaces; knocking glasses off the face; head butting; throwing food from or standing up in a high chair. I have observed all these behaviors in hundreds of perfectly normal, nicely developing nine- to fourteen-month-old children.

Bad habits begin to develop at the same time and for exactly the same reasons as good habits. When a babe-in-arms playfully or accidentally knocks the glasses off her parent's face, the response is predictably quick and dramatic. The parent usually makes a noise, moves swiftly to catch the glasses, and puts on a look of annoyance. Very few parents enjoy having the frame of their glasses dig into their nose or having their glasses knocked to the floor. The baby certainly has attracted their full attention.

Take biting as another example. Babies of this age are typically teething. Their gums are usually somewhat sensitive, so biting down on hard plastic objects is very common and apparently pleasurable. Sometimes in the course of harmless gumming a baby may bite down firmly on a parent's arm or shoulder. This can really hurt, and the parent's surprised reaction is usually immediate and dramatic. This is the way a child's bad habits get reinforced in the period between seven and one-half and eleven months.

Bad habits fall into three categories: interpersonal, such as biting or hitting; anxiety-provoking, such as standing up on a rocking chair or reaching for an electric cord; and potentially destructive or expensive, such as exploring a treasured plant or a new CD player. What they have in common is that your baby has seen that certain actions get a dramatic rise out of you. That kind of response from you is exciting to your baby and worth trying again!

## LEARNING TO INSIST ON GETTING ONE'S WAY

Several of the social developments that are first clearly seen in the period from seven and one-half months to fourteen months can be characterized as the emergence of the baby's capacity to exert his personal force—or throw his weight around. While it is true that a four-month-old child may scream and rage, such displeasure clearly is not directed toward another human being. On the other hand, when an eight-month-old baby resists being fed or diapered, or engages in a more benign activity such as initiating a game of peek-a-boo, he clearly is aiming this behavior at the person with whom he is interacting.

The exciting experience of finding that your parents get a big kick out of some of the things you do is followed, toward the end of the first year, by a new kind of behavior: initiating games. Having experienced many episodes where making a funny face or turning themselves in a circle while sitting on the floor was followed by a big response from their parents, eleven- or twelve-month-old babies may very well make a funny face or start to make themselves dizzy, then pause and look for a grand reaction.

In this manner, as the weeks go by, the child approaching one year of age begins to exercise initiative in social situations. This initiative is part of a lengthy and significant evolution. During the second year it will take the more forceful form of insisting that a parent do what the child dictates. We call that behavior "directing." During the third year, that kind of executive ability, developed in play with her parents at home, enables the child to begin to experiment with leadership with peers. The ability to lead another child (as well as to give that child an equal chance to lead you) is one of the eight distinguishing social abilities of the outstanding three- to six-year-old child. Outstanding six-year-olds are comfortable in either role. Others are comfortable only when they lead but do not enjoy taking turns at leading. Still others only seem comfortable in the role of follower. Of course, many six-year-olds are so socially inhibited that they can neither lead nor follow another child.

I believe that the origins of leadership can be found in this rich seven-and-one-half-to-fourteen-month period of life.

When a lovely one-year-old initiates games, it's lots of fun for everyone. Unfortunately, babies begin to experiment with throwing their weight around in ways that not only are not fun but that usually create a fair amount of stress in typical families. The principal example of this is using the cry to insist on getting their own way.

Your baby will insist on getting his way under two sets of conditions: In the feeding situation, he will at times resist your direction (and, in a sense, your authority). In the other kind of situation, your child will want to do something over your objections. You should expect both kinds of events to happen more and more often between seven and one-half and fourteen months. How much of this behavior your baby continues to engage in at fourteen months of age depends directly on how you handle the situation during those six and one-half months. Remember, all normal babies go through this process during this stage of life.

The way you respond to your baby's attempts to use power and to express her desires through the cry during these six and one-half months determines what kind of fourteen-month-old child you are going to be living with. The range of outcomes is surprisingly broad, and the consequences are substantial.

Babies also practice complaining to the key people in their lives when they don't like what is happening on the changing table.

## The Remarkable Significance of What the Nine- to Twelve-Month-Old Learns During Diapering

Normal infants between ten and fourteen months of age *hate* to be diapered. You can count on your baby to use all means at her disposal to complain during diapering. She will resist the situation with physical action, she will try to roll out of your grip, she may arch her back to escape your grip, she may even kick you. All this behavior (and more) is common. I have often seen parents give up the changing table and follow their babies around, trying to diaper them while the infant continues to move away. (By the way, that kind of diapering style may continue throughout the second year of life!) That method of coping with the baby's resistance hardly ever works out well.

Babies will also make use of every type of cry in their repertoire to object to diapering. At times the resistance is because their skin is irritated and the cleaning process causes pain. Far more commonly, however, the basis for their unhappiness over diapering is that they cannot stand being pinned down or held firmly, even for a few seconds!

As the baby's resistance to diapering grows, parents try several tactics in order to cope. Distraction is one of the first. With an eight-month-old, distraction is much more likely to work than with a one-year-old. Early success with offering the objecting eight-month-old a small toy or mirror sadly doesn't last long. Day by day, the resistance increases.

Parents almost always try to talk their babies into going along with diapering. The parent delivers a steady stream of words intended to calm and soothe the baby. Interestingly, if the baby is in the midst of resisting the process, this tactic usually has an effect opposite to what the parent intends. The baby resists more fiercely. The words that are intended to console reinforce the resistance.

Fierce struggles over diapering can disappear before fourteen months of age or can continue at least until the second birthday. The difference appears to depend directly on how parents handle the situation. Later I will describe how you can turn this inevitably difficult situation into an invaluable opportunity as you guide a baby into a healthy balance between the legitimate expression of his needs and throwing a fit when he can't have his way.

## The Balance Among Principal Interests

During the beginning of the period from seven and one-half to fourteen months, all healthy babies are motivated by their physical needs, such as those for food or comfort, as well as by three major interests: social interactions, mastery of the body, and satisfaction of curiosity. At seven and one-half months of age, each of the primary interests is quite strong, and the three are in balance. As time goes by, the balance is sometimes lost.

In the case of one family we worked with, the physical space available for the newly crawling eight-month-old child was very limited. It consisted principally of a very small, quite cluttered living room. The kitchen was immediately off the living room, but the mother would not let the baby roam there for fear of an accident. In addition, the mother spent the majority of the time all week long with her child.

The child's orientation toward his mother grew at a more rapid rate than is typical. Day after day, he became increasingly demanding of her attention. As he got better at climbing, he was all over her like a blanket. She was being smothered. From previous experience, we knew they were headed for trouble. The baby's interests in mastering his body and in exploring the physical world were being starved. The only game in town was his mother. This kind of inadvertant compression of a baby's experiences is common (and easily prevented).

In other instances, we've observed babies in this age range whose parents were both working full-time out of the home; someone had been hired to see to it that the baby was safe and to maintain the home (clean, cook, do laundry). In one such situation, I remember that the person who was taking care of the child had very little interest in the baby. The result was that the child spent the bulk of the day in a state of social isolation in his own home. When the parents were at home in the evening and on weekends, there was a good deal of interaction, but for the majority of his waking hours throughout the week, this child had an extremely different pattern of experiences from that of the child who has a parent or a grandparent with him much of the time.

When you consider what I've been describing as the remarkable richness of social developments during this period, clearly the outcome at fourteen months of age can be markedly influenced by the family's general lifestyle as well as their particular style of behavior in direct interactions with the baby.

Two other common parenting decisions that have important effects on the balance of primary interests and the social development of the child have to do with whether the child is allowed to roam through the home and whether she is allowed to pursue the universally powerful interest in climbing. We always caution the families we work with that from the beginning of this period on through to at least twenty months of age, there are two major sources of serious accidents in a child's life. The first is accidental poisonings; the second is falls from high places. Parents of course have to be careful about these genuine threats. Some parents, however, become unusually fearful about the possibility of accidents and severely limit the child's opportunity to explore the home. They especially limit the child's opportunity to climb stairs, chairs, furniture, and even toys designed for the purpose.

To sum up, the seven-and-one-half-to-fourteen-month period of life ushers in a time of remarkable richness and importance in the social development process. Not only are the events of this time of life fascinating, but it is highly likely that they have major, lasting effects on the shaping of a baby's personality. These effects very probably are considerably greater than those that result from congenital factors, though I confess that I cannot prove that statement. The experiences of these six and one-half months also have major, direct consequences for the tone of everyday family life both during the period and for the balance of the second year of life. From seven and one-half months on, everyone finds the excitement and pleasures growing steadily. When development does not go well, however, this can be a time of growing stress and dissatisfaction.

The direction of a baby's social interest during this period is exclusively toward his parents, except if there is an older sibling in the home and the spacing is less than three years. In such situations, parents have to be prepared for a dramatic increase in sibling rivalry and stress on everyone involved.

Several other important changes are taking place during this time. It is the most likely time in life for the appearance of both stranger anxiety and separation anxiety, conditions that usually only last two months or so. Yet this is also a very rich time with respect to the acquisition of important social abilities: using an adult as a resource, expressing affection and annoyance to adults, showing pride in achievement, and engaging in make-believe play.

A baby's social style begins to take shape during this period. She begins to exhibit enjoyment in getting the key people in her life to laugh or to praise her. She also begins to learn what annoys them. She learns what different cries lead to. She acquires a repertoire of social habits, some delightful, some not delightful. She learns a lot from the diapering experience. She learns whether throwing a fit will get her what she wants when there has been resistance to that. Finally, she may get used to a life that consists of many opportunities to satisfy her curiosity and to practice hand-eye skills and climbing. She may spend a good deal of time every day in the company of the key people in her life, or she may experience any number of variations in living conditions, including ones where she is usually in the company of a few or several other children. If she has an older brother or sister and the age gap is less than three years, her social life will have been more complicated than if she were a first child. While she surely will have had some loving experiences with her older sibling, she will just as surely have been on the receiving end of a considerable number of acts of jealousy and aggression. Sad to say, she will have learned more about fear of another small person than would otherwise have been the case.

## HOW THE PROCESS CAN GO WRONG

By seven and one-half months, the biggest problem loving parents may have to cope with is a baby who has a well-established habit of demanding attention all day long, every day. Along with an overdeveloped need for attention, that baby will probably have slightly less curiosity than he might have developed. Both less-than-ideal qualities are the result of what usually happens during the preceeding two months when parents are unaware of how to provide a rich set of options for their pre-crawling baby.

Although development may not have been ideal up to that point, once the baby begins to crawl the situation can easily be corrected; on the other hand, it often becomes considerably worse. In the balance of this chapter I will deal with why things go poorly and how to avoid the pitfalls.

I have been describing three major social developments: the baby's evolving interest in people, her social abilities, and the shaping of her social style. During this period of life, your baby's interest in you can begin to overwhelm her other primary interests: mastering and enjoying her body and satisfying her curiosity about the world. The development of social abilities is not very likely to be a problem, but the development of her social style is very much at risk.

---

## How the Interest in People Can Get Out of Hand

It is common for an infant to become excessively oriented toward his mother during the last half of his first year. Here are the reasons why.

## What Kind of Parenting Style Do You Adopt When Your Baby Learns to Crawl?

About three-quarters of all children begin to be able to move across a room by about seven and one-half months of age. One in 500 can crawl at five months. Some normal babies can't until they're quite a bit older, as late as ten or eleven months. Other skip crawling altogether and move from pulling to sit to pulling to stand to cruising and walking. None of these differences has anything to do with subsequent intellectual growth, but they do have substantial consequences for daily life and for social development.

Naturally, parents become quite excited when they see that their baby can crawl. Soon after the excitement quiets down, they have to decide what to do about the consequences of that new ability. The child's crawling efforts don't represent sophisticated athletic ability but are a rather shaky proposition at first. Babies of this age still don't know the difference between things that are safe to put in the mouth, like nipples and bottles and food, and those that are not, like electric cords and objects they can choke on. Almost everything that is portable will be brought to the mouth. It soon becomes obvious that a newly crawling baby is in danger of hurting herself and that the danger becomes even greater when the baby starts to climb.

It also soon becomes clear that a newly crawling baby is a danger not only to herself but also to any breakable objects in the home. Her curiosity has no limits, but her knowledge and delicacy do. Babies of this age destroy plants, dishes, television and radio mechanisms, and more. They love to put small objects into dark places, and the slot that accepts video cassettes is just right for the purpose. Many families have lost car keys, jewelry, and other important objects in VCRs and heating registers.

Another inevitable consequence of a free-crawling infant is more housework. Ashtrays and trash baskets are for tipping. Shelves full of books and records are for emptying. Newspapers and magazines are for tearing. Yet another difficulty will develop if your baby has a slightly older sibling. Your younger child will begin to get on your older child's nerves. Sibling rivalry begins to be a daily problem once your baby reaches this stage and requires more attention from you—and also wants to explore his older sister's possessions.

Parents faced with these new conditions of genuine danger, potential extra expense, and increases in workload have to decide what to do. By and large, you have two alternatives: Either take precautions and let your child roam, or keep him confined to places where he can't cause you grief.

One common style parents use is to limit the baby's range. This is done in any number of ways. Some parents use playpens as a routine place to put the baby throughout the day. Others use the crib from the end of breakfast to the beginning of lunch, from the end of lunch until the beginning of supper, and then from the end of supper until bedtime. That practice is more common than you might think, particularly if the family doesn't have much money. Another approach is to put the baby in a small room filled with toys and then place a gate at the doorway to keep the child there for most of the day. I have seen jump seats placed in front of television sets, corrals set up around the baby, and tethering mechanisms with harnesses. Parents use many methods with the same goal in mind: Don't let that child roam.

Other parents, in spite of the danger and extra work, wouldn't think of confining their newly mobile baby. They encourage her explorations. This style of parenting requires that they modify the home so that it becomes safe *for* the

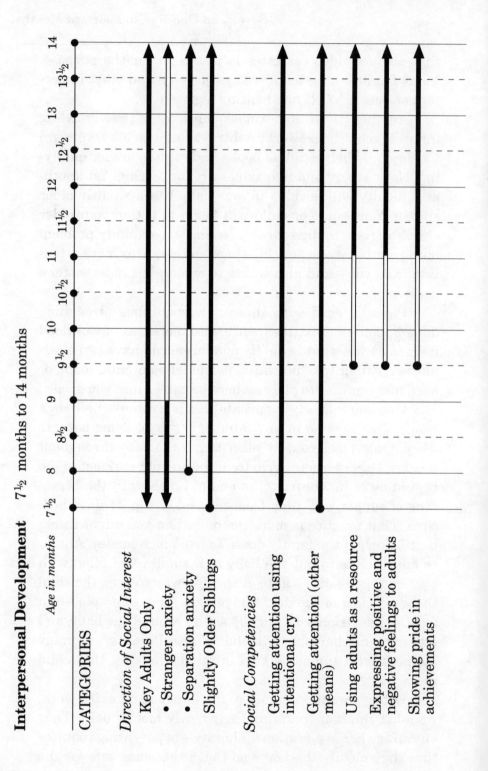

**Interpersonal Development**  7½ months to 14 months

*Age in months*

14  13½  13  12½  12  11½  11  10½  10  9½  9  8½  8  7½

CATEGORIES

*Direction of Social Interest*

Key Adults Only

• Stranger anxiety

• Separation anxiety

Slightly Older Siblings

*Social Competencies*

Getting attention using
intentional cry

Getting attention (other
means)

Using adults as a resource

Expressing positive and
negative feelings to adults

Showing pride in
achievements

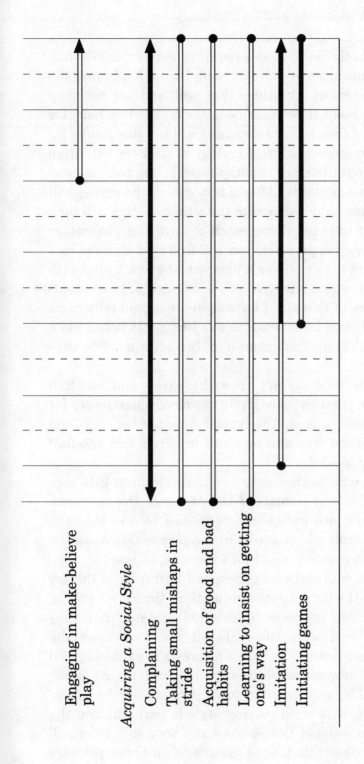

Engaging in make-believe play

*Acquiring a Social Style*

Complaining

Taking small mishaps in stride

Acquisition of good and bad habits

Learning to insist on getting one's way

Imitation

Initiating games

baby and *from* the baby. It also requires more supervision.

If you encourage a baby to roam through a home, she will find all sorts of situations that will feed her curiosity and keep her busy. If you confine a newly crawling baby for long periods of time to a playpen, she will not stay happy for long. You can expect a lot of crying, at first for attention and, increasingly, to show unhappiness. Young babies, however, are very adaptable. After a few weeks, the crying will lessen and your baby will accept the situation. She will then spend a lot of time not doing much of anything. No matter how many toys you give her, you will find that if she is routinely confined to her crib or a playpen, she won't play with any toy for very long. To give you some idea of how adaptable babies are at this age, I have seen them gradually come to accept daily two-hour sessions in a jump seat in front of a television set! They don't complain, but after a while they just fall asleep!

The baby who doesn't crawl by seven and one-half months of age is much more likely to overdevelop the cry for company simply because the typical period of boredom and frustration—from five and one-half to seven and one-half months—is extended.

Parents who've chosen to put their children into confined areas for long periods of the day once the baby can crawl generally are somewhat distressed to find that the child won't simply play happily in the playpen. Instead the child will continue to cry out for attention, at least at first. Some parents will continue to respond faithfully to the cry and find that the baby's demands on their time grow day by day. (In fact, they get to be considerably greater than they would have been were the child allowed to explore the home.) In other words, the baby's interests in exploring and in practicing new motor skills such as climbing are being suppressed. The only game in town is to cry out for attention. In effect, this child-rearing style is perpetuating the situation that existed before the baby was able to crawl! Instead of a steady, balanced growth of all three primary interests, this style of child-rearing leads a baby to concentrate his attention on his social life (usually his mother). As a result, these six and one-half months get to be much more difficult for parents than they have to be.

## WHY THE DEVELOPMENT OF SPECIAL SOCIAL ABILITIES IS NOT AT RISK AT THIS POINT

The five important social abilities that develop during the first fourteen months of life require only regular contact with parents or grandparents to emerge and develop well. When a ten-month-old gestures that she wants more juice or crackers (tries to use an adult as a resource), most parents will notice the request and provide what is being asked for. Except under unusual conditions, babies at this stage begin to ask for food or help and usually get it. Likewise, when a baby takes his first steps, parents and grandparents are invariably delighted and show it, and in the process begin to nurture the baby's emerging pride in achievement.

The only way any of the special abilities will fail to develop is if adults consistently neglect a baby during the first two years of life. The initial development of special social abilities usually goes well even when a baby is developing into an overindulged child.

## HOW AN UNDESIRABLE SOCIAL STYLE BEGINS TO FORM

Since, more than anything else, how you deal with the three critical social lessons of this period will determine what kind of social style your baby will have at fourteen months of age, let me describe the common errors you should avoid.

## Crying After a Minor Accident

Once crawling starts, at seven and one-half months (slightly before if the child is practicing getting to a sitting position on his own), babies start to suffer garden-variety bumps and bruises. They fall down a lot, they bump their heads, they squeeze their fingers. Any number of non-life-threatening but definitely painful experiences begin to become more numerous. The common response to these episodes is the cry.

During the first months of their baby's life, parents have to respond quickly and compassionately to the frequent cries of their baby, to relieve her discomfort, and to help her begin to build healthy emotional foundations and good feelings about people. That vital response style usually becomes well established within a few weeks. The overreactive style I described in connection with the minor bumps and bruises of the newly crawling baby is actually a continuation of what I strongly advocate during the baby's first months of life. But if parents continue to respond to their eight- or nine-month-old in a similar way, the baby is very likely to develop a habit of excessive crying. As the child leaves the first six months of life, parents have to modify how they behave in response to their baby's cries. Perhaps because those early months are so exciting, some parents have trouble with the transition.

Some parents, especially those who are exceptionally soft-hearted and have excellent hearing ability, will react to all such crying episodes immediately, regardless of the level of discomfort. They hear the cry, drop what they're doing, and move quickly to the child and try to comfort her. This usually involves picking her up and moving her gently back and forth, patting her back, perhaps even using a pacifier. It also includes some soothing words. This common style of response to the numerous, everyday minor accidents of this stage of life reinforces the crying behavior. It is one of several classic ways in which the baby is taught by her parents to cry as a habitual response to a wide variety of events. The direct consequence of this overreactive style of parenting is that as the eighth and ninth months of life go by, the baby steadily increases the frequency and duration of her cries.

Compounding this problem is the emergence of stranger and separation anxiety during the same period.

As you might expect, a certain amount of crying because of stranger or separation anxiety is to be expected at this stage. However, the baby whose parents have been over-reacting to her minor accidents will begin to overreact to these classic sources of distress as well. By one year of age, such a baby cries at the least provocation and sometimes for no obvious reason! Living with that kind of a "crybaby" is no fun at all.

## The Development of Bad Habits

Babies in this remarkable period from seven and one-half to fourteen months often acquire several annoying habits. Most parents haven't the faintest idea of how these habits developed or what to do about them. A typical response when the baby engages in one of these annoying behaviors is for the parent to say (with increasing firmness) "No, you mustn't do that!" It is true that from about eight to nine months on, babies do begin to perceive (with some small degree of acknowledgment) their parents' disapproval. That does not mean that that disapproval is effective in preventing or eliminating bad habits. It generally is not. In fact, such verbal scolding is counterproductive! It actually reinforces the unwanted behavior, since as a parent scolds a nine-month-old the baby seems to appreciate having the adult's full attention.

• • •

## How Learning to Insist on Having Your Way Can Get Out of Hand

The final area where the process can go awry during the period from seven and one-half to fourteen months is in respect to the development of the child's capacity to insist on getting her own way. As mentioned earlier, this process surfaces generally during the seventh month in connection with mealtimes and diaperings. It also frequently becomes a problem at nap times and bedtimes.

### INSISTING ON GETTING YOUR WAY WHEN IT IS TIME TO GO TO SLEEP

Once babies learn that crying will bring Mom or Dad to their crib, they begin to use the cry for that purpose at nap times, bedtimes, and late at night. The seven-month-old baby has usually settled into a fairly regular sleep pattern: bedtime between seven-thirty and eight-thirty at night, sleeping through until five-thirty to seven o'clock in the morning. They have also begun to take two naps a day. There are plenty of exceptions, but in general a regular (and civilized) sleep pattern is usually in place by seven months of age.

Many seven-months-old babies begin to object to being put down to sleep, particularly if parents are going by the clock rather than by sleep signs. This resistance is especially true of babies who are beginning to overuse their cry to insist on getting their own way. Day by day, they get better at using that tool promptly and effectively. The baby is taken into her room and put into her crib, and she begins to cry. The cry escalates quickly to intense levels. Within a month or so the baby has learned that a scream will bring faster action from a parent than a soft or moderately loud cry. Parents then take the baby out of the crib after two or three minutes. The baby is weepy but starts to play again. Shortly, a second attempt is made to put her to sleep. The baby complains again, and this becomes a regular, difficult pattern.

The same pattern can and will occur, in some cases, at two or three in the morning when the child awakens because of some minor disturbance and, finding it dark and quiet, uses the only tool that he has in order to change the situation. He cries for his mother. Unfortunately, two-thirty in the morning is not a convenient time for his parents, but that doesn't have much meaning to a seven-month-old.

## THE FIRST STRUGGLE FOR POWER

When parents have not managed to set limits effectively during the nine-to twelve-month period, the testing behavior of the baby takes on a much less tentative quality by the first birthday. By then the baby is beginning to get out of control. While some testing continues, much of it has begun to develop into an early struggle for power. With such a baby, the second year of life steadily becomes more difficult. The testing turns into demands for attention. The baby has learned that when he tests, he gets attention immediately and reliably. Testing becomes a control tool. This development becomes very obvious when the parents of such a baby try to hold a conversation with other people while the baby is nearby. You can expect such a child to insist on attention after a few minutes and to use previously disapproved behavior if that attention isn't given quickly. He has learned that certain behaviors will almost always work.

## SUMMARY

What kind of child do you have at fourteen months of age if you've inadvertently fallen into some of the traps that I've been describing? At fourteen months and ten days, Cheryl had a well-ingrained behavior at dinnertime that really bothered her parents. If Daddy wasn't going to feed her, nobody would. If her mother attempted to feed her, Cheryl would immediately start screaming, crying real tears and in general looking as if she was moving into a hysterical state. The fact that she would scream immediately was a clear sign that such behavior had been around for some time. Since we had been working with the family for several months, we knew that this was so. You have to ask yourself in this situation, as in many other situations, is there any conceivable reason why a baby has to be fed by her father? The answer is quite obvious, yet what we were dealing with was a typical case of a child who had been taught that if she screamed, she would get what she wanted.

In this case, to be fair to the parents, not only were they totally in love with their child, but the child had been born prematurely, and the parents had been cautioned that premature babies were somewhat more at risk than full-term babies. The child was also slightly underweight. Her parents were therefore especially concerned that the child get enough to eat and, most important, that she not develop any kind of eating disorder. This made the task more difficult for them than for others. I can assure you, however, that many parents of full-term, perfectly healthy children can end up with the same sort of problems at dinnertime.

Another baby of about the same age who used her surprising power equally effectively was Dolly, a charming, energetic little girl. Her parents also used an especially accommodating style in dealing with her many episodes of insisting on getting her way. During a home visit with Dolly, her mother and I were sitting on the sofa. Her father was sitting on a low plastic double seat. Dolly was moving around the room from place to place and object to object while making regular attempts to get attention from each of her parents. After ten minutes or so, Dolly went over to her father and began to push him in the direction of the adjacent empty seat. At first he wasn't sure what she wanted, but when he got the message he moved. After no more than ten seconds, Dolly, who had positioned herself in the vacated seat, got up, walked around to her father's other side, and began to push him back to his original seat. This act was repeated with her father's puzzled cooperation eight or nine times over a ten-minute span. Interestingly, no humor was shown by either party. Moreover, Dolly's father was mildly unhappy because the behavior was making it difficult for us to carry on a discussion.

Dolly's father, like most, loved his daughter dearly. He let Dolly prolong her "directing" partly because of his own gentle personality and partly because he didn't know how much of such behavior was within ordinary, acceptable limits. In Dolly's case, as is usual, this episode was typical of much of her daily behavior and also the parenting style of her parents. She was much "pushier" than most fourteen-month-olds, and they were much more indulgent than more successful parents.

As an isolated incident, such "pushy" behavior wouldn't mean much. In our experience, however, such behavior in a fourteen-month-old is never isolated but invariably reflects a social style that had evolved during the period of life from seven and one-half-months to fourteen months.

Then there was Sam, another powerhouse personality at fourteen months of age, who enjoyed the first time he was allowed to sit in his father's lap during dinnertime. Each night over the next week, Sam would ask to sit on his father's lap while eating and would be allowed to do so. Sam not only enjoyed the arrangement but began to insist on it, and what a fuss he would put up if there was resistance! At first his father thought the behavior was cute, but gradually he came to feel annoyed at not being able to eat a meal in comfort. Sam, on the other hand, made it crystal clear that this was the way it was going to be. In this case, it was not all that difficult for us to convince his parents that Sam was gradually becoming a bully and going beyond his legitimate rights. With our help, the behavior was discouraged. It took about four days for Sam to get accustomed to the notion that he had to be in his own chair at dinnertime. During that time, he complained a lot. And by the way, he continued to love both parents every bit as much as when they had been overindulging him.

You might say that these families should have known better than to condone such behaviors, that they should have used their common sense. Most first-time parents, however, have neither the necessary perspective nor the objectivity needed to avoid the development of such behavior or to be able to reverse it easily.

Bullying, crying twenty times more often in the course of the day than the average child, and a collection of unpleasant habits, such as biting, hitting, hair pulling, and frequent complaining—these are the classic signs in the fourteen-month-old of a child whose social development has moved into a direction that forecasts trouble for the child at three years of age. I hate to say it, but innocence—as in the innocence of a baby—is gone by the first birthday. Spoiling, in the specific sense that I have just described, is not at all uncommon by fourteen months of age; frankly, if it is well established by then, it is very difficult to undo. In social terms, a fourteen-month-old baby is no longer young!

## A SURPRISING AND IMPORTANT FACT ABOUT EXPLANATIONS AND THE SEVEN-AND-ONE-HALF- TO FOURTEEN-MONTH-OLD CHILD

At the beginning of the seven-and-one-half-to-fourteen-month period, most babies are doing well if they understand one or two words. By fourteen months, the average baby understands two to three dozen. Concepts such as "danger" or "fairness" or "sharing" or "refugees starving in another country," however, are all more than babies of that age can understand. And, of course, babies don't deal with patterns of words in sentences very well. Clearly, then, their capacity to understand language is quite limited. Nonetheless, for obvious reasons, that doesn't prevent some parents from attempting to use a lot of talk in trying to console their unhappy baby.

The tendency to try to console an unhappy infant through explaining that "it is not going to last long—it will only hurt for a moment—Mommy needs to do this" is totally understandable, and indeed with older children and adults often successful. When you are trying to set limits with a baby between seven and one-half months and two years of age, however, explanations are actually counterproductive. Throughout this developmental period, explanations not only do not work, they actually reinforce the undesirable behavior.

The reason seems to be that while you're explaining something to a baby he is aware that he has your total attention. Especially during the eight-to-twenty-four-month period, the full attention of a parent is an extremely powerful reinforcer. As long as the baby has your attention because you are talking to her, pouring your heart out trying to make her feel better, she will continue to struggle as you try to diaper her or will continue to try to grab your glasses.

This style of parenting, featuring explanations delivered on a regular basis by an increasingly frustrated parent, is not at all rare. It is a style often adopted with first children by especially loving, intelligent, and soft-hearted parents who tend to use a good deal of language in their daily lives.

Now that I have described how loving parents with the best of intentions can go wrong during this special period, let's look at what does work well.

• • •

## HOW TO GUIDE YOUR BABY THROUGH THE FIRST DIFFICULT STAGE OF SOCIAL DEVELOPMENT

### Goals

What I'm hoping your baby will be like at fourteen months of age is as follows:

A child whose three major interests—satisfying her curiosity, developing and enjoying motor skills, and enjoying social interactions—are each strong and in balance with the others.

A child who does not overuse the cry, who has learned to take minor setbacks and discomforts in stride.

A child free from annoying habits such as biting, hair pulling, knocking glasses off, and hitting.

A child who has learned that she has the right to repeat herself slightly more forcefully when she really wants something very much or really does not want to go along with something that's been proposed to her, or when she hasn't been understood. After the child has repeated her message once and perhaps with slightly greater intensity and it has been made clear to her that she cannot have her way, she should in most situations cease and desist and go along with your authority.

A child who accepts being diapered.

A happy child, who obviously is having a wonderful time in life and rarely complains or cries unless she is experiencing significant physical discomfort.

How do you achieve these goals?

## 1) Maintaining the Balance Among the Primary Interests

Aside from the newly crawling baby's physical need for food, sleep, and comfort, we observed early on in our research that most of what he engages in serves one of three primary interests. If you examine what your baby does in the course of the day, you'll find he is either trying to interact with people (the social interest), improving or enjoying his newly developing physical skills (the motor interest), or exploring (satisfying his curiosity). The typical newly crawling baby enjoys vigorously pursuing each of these three interests.

The nicely developed three-year-old continues to have equally strong interests in each of these three directions. By way of contrast, the child who is neglected or treated harshly may very well have a depressed social interest while still maintaining some curiosity and interest in using his body. More commonly, particularly with a first child in a loving home, the imbalance involves an overdevelopment of the social interest at the expense of the others. Clingy, whiney two-year-olds would fall into this category. Likewise, a child at seven months of age who had been regularly bored and frustrated in the preceding couple of months is very likely to cry and insist on being picked up much more than if he had had a variety of interesting things to do during that earlier time.

In the last section, I introduced the concept of designing a developmentally suitable world for the five-and-one-half-month-old baby in order to hold down boredom and frustration and to discourage the overuse of the intentional cry for company. Once a baby can crawl across a room with ease, the task of holding down excessive demands for attention becomes even easier. It starts with safety-proofing the home.

• • •

## SAFETY-PROOFING THE HOME

If you have made use of a walker, you have already begun to safety-proof your home. When your baby is about six months old, you have to do more extensive safety-proofing because she may begin to crawl and climb at any time. I urge you to make it possible for your newly crawling child to explore as much of your home as possible. If you allow her to do so, safety-proofing is essential. You can learn a fair amount about this subject by reading the appropriate sections in *The First Three Years of Life,* and several other good books are available that provide guidance on the subject. There also are now companies that will provide a free evaluation of your home. They make their money by selling you such devices as safety latches for cabinets, electric outlet closures, stair gates, and so on. (The most recent fee one of our families paid for such service in their three-bedroom ranch-style house was $500, but you don't have to spend anything like that kind of money to make your home safe.)

For the new crawler, you have to pay particular attention to the area within two feet or so of the floor. Later, as her climbing ability increases, you will have to extend your efforts to higher levels.

In addition to general safety-proofing, we recommend a gate at the top of all stairways, and another on the lip of the third step from the bottom. We also suggest some cushioning on the floor at the foot of the stairs. Finally, a simple hook-and-eye latch should be placed high on every bathroom door and be kept latched unless an adult is in the bathroom. Last, but far from least, as many kitchen cabinets and pantry spaces as possible should be made safe and available to the seven-and-one-half- to fourteen-month-old child.

If you take these steps and become knowledgeable about the evolution of interests and abilities of the child during this period, you will be well on the way toward designing a developmentally suitable physical environment for the child.

## ALLOWING EXPLORATION OF AS MUCH OF THE HOME AS POSSIBLE

The next step in the process is to turn her loose! Your child will require no inducements to explore. In the process of doing so, she will find generous sources for satisfying her curiosity and for feeding her interest in mastering and enjoying her body. She will also begin to learn a good deal about the key people in her life, far more than she ever would if she spent lots of time in a playpen or in a room filled with toys but with a gate in the doorway. This will happen, by the way, whether your home is a mansion or very simple. To a newly crawling baby, any home is a wonderland.

There is one more essential ingredient: the presence, for the majority of the baby's waking hours, of someone who is crazy about the child, probably you.

No factor is more essential for good results in nourishing the baby's excitement in learning than the regular presence of someone who loves her. *Nevertheless, from seven and one-half months on, I recommend that neither parent be at home with a baby full-time.* I suggest that full-time parents spend a few hours a day out of the home, away from the child. You may be able to hire a sensible, caring teenager at low cost in order to achieve that goal. The point is that interrupting the continuity of contact between baby and parent will help keep the social relationship from becoming too intense. In turn, it becomes easier to encourage the baby's interests in satisfying her curiosity about the rest of the world and in perfecting her newly emerging motor skills.

Of course, introducing another person into your baby's daily life at this stage has to be done with due regard for the possibility of some stranger and separation anxiety. Introducing the new person early on, even during the seventh month of life, works well. A good idea for the first few weeks is to have the babysitter spend most of her time with the baby at your home. At this age, infants are more secure there than anywhere else.

## 2) Teaching a Child to Take Minor Difficulties in Stride

Crying over small matters is not something you need worry about before the baby is seven and one-half months old (and sixteen or seventeen months of age is too late). You have to expect that a newly crawling baby who will soon be pulling herself to stand and climbing to greater and greater heights is going to fall and bump herself many times in the course of a week. Your task is to make sure that the baby learns that while you care about her discomfort, she should be expected to bear up under short-lived, slight pain and then move on. Of course, if there's a fall and you hear a particularly intense cry, you should go to the baby quickly and try to comfort her as well as you can. In such situations, it is far more important to show your concern than it is to worry about overindulgence.

The vast majority of falls, however, will lead to cries that, though more than minimal, will end before you can count to twenty, provided you don't get into the habit of dropping everything and rushing to the baby at every such occurrence. My advice is: Note whether the cry is minimal or intense. If you're sure the baby is really hurting or if you are in doubt, react quickly by going to the baby and trying to comfort him immediately. If, as is far more common, he seems to be experiencing only mild discomfort, respond verbally only by saying something to show that you have noticed his cry and that you are sorry and then count to twenty (slowly, now) to see if indeed it will blow over. In most cases, it will. Remember, your attention is an extremely powerful reinforcer during the early months of a child's life. Behaving in a caring but, at appropriate times, matter-of-fact manner is the best way to teach a baby to take minor mishaps in stride. If you manage to do this part of the job well, I promise you won't have a crybaby at fourteen months of age.

•  •  •

## 3) Preventing the Development of Bad Habits

This particular goal is more difficult to attain than the first two. Dealing with it requires two kinds of treatments, prevention and remediation. Clearly, if you can prevent the development of a biting, head-butting, or hair-pulling child, that's your best outcome.

Starting when your child is seven months old, you should be mindful of the possibility of the development of certain common bad habits. If you have long hair or wear glasses or earrings, you should expect that your baby will want to explore them, in the process possibly hurting you or damaging the glasses. When you pick him up, keep an eye on whether he begins to stare at your glasses, fumble for your hair, or eye your earrings. Such behaviors are inevitable with any normal baby, who is brimming with curiosity and interest in hand-eye explorations. You might consider several options: You could remove your glasses before you pick him up, wear your hair up for a few months, give up earrings for a few months.

If you can't avoid a painful yank on your hair, try to adopt the following coping style. Do your darnedest to avoid an immediate, dramatic response. Try not to cry out quickly and loudly. That kind of perfectly natural style of response is reinforcing to a baby of this age. It is particularly noticeable in the case of a baby attempting to knock eyeglasses off a parent's face. The parent's usual response clearly leads to repetition of the behavior, and after a dozen or so times, it becomes habitual. If your baby manages to get a grip on your hair, reach for her hand and firmly disentangle it, while telling her, in simple language and with a serious look on your face, not to pull hair. By seven and one-half months of age, babies are beginning to be able to sense your disapproval. They begin to learn the meaning of the word "no," and they begin to become aware of the new tone of serious disapproval in your voice, along with a new look on your face.

From this time on, some parents begin to adopt the habit of lengthy, heartfelt explanations when attempting to control their baby. I can understand the inclination, but I have become convinced that these attempts seriously interfere with achieving the best results when socializing a child. The idea of telling a nine-month-old that when she pulls your hair you feel pain and that she may actually extract some hair and that hair pulling is antisocial may feel right to you as an adult, but at this age (a) the baby won't understand more than one or two words and (b) the overlong explanation actually reinforces the undesirable behavior. After all, while you're saying all of those things your baby has your full attention.

Of one thing you can be sure when an annoying habit becomes established during the last few months of the first year of life: The reason invariably is that one or both parents, usually unwittingly, have been reinforcing the behavior. Awareness is the basis of prevention, and prevention is better than having to remediate.

What do you do if your best efforts fail to prevent the development of a bad habit or two, or three, or more? That depends on the habit. Be aware that at this stage of development, anything your baby does that gets a rise out of you may very well become habitual. If your baby repeatedly drops food to the floor and stands up in his high chair, my advice is to end the meal, even if the meal has just begun. If you end the meal, don't resume it a few minutes later or you will delay the elimination of the habit. Also, don't worry that your child will become malnourished. When babies need food, they need no encouragement to eat. You should repeat your admonishment only once. If that doesn't work, end the meal. Again, do not use elaborate explanations.

· · ·

## DISCIPLINE: GETTING RID OF A BAD HABIT—
## RESTRICTION OF MOVEMENT

If a bad habit involves doing something to another person that causes pain, such as biting or hair pulling, you have to make the price of the bad habit too high. The procedure we recommend is based on our observation that most healthy ten- to twelve-month-old children object vigorously when you try to hold them still, even briefly. Even those who will hold still for diapering are not at all happy when their movements are restricted.

If a baby insists upon biting you and you have said "no" twice, it is time to raise the price. Pick the baby up and move her across the room or into another room. Sit down and hold her in front of you, facing you, while at the same time holding her shoulders and upper arms. Don't squeeze her shoulders, but hold her firmly enough so that she cannot move so much as an eighth of an inch. Don't be surprised if she looks at you and smiles or laughs. Your job is to try not to laugh back at her. If the child simply stays in place for two, three, or four minutes and doesn't complain, you're allowing too much movement. If you're holding her firmly enough, after a minute or two she will start to indicate that she doesn't like what's happening. At that point, take a look at your watch, but continue to hold her in this way for fifteen seconds more. The baby will complain more and more. At the end of fifteen seconds, make a very brief speech. Say something like, "We're going to go back into the other room now and we will play but if you bite me again, I'm going to do this again." (Of course, she won't understand many of the words, but that isn't necessary.) That's all. No warnings about infections or damage to the epidermis, just a short, sweet setting of a limit from which you will not budge. Our experience has demonstrated repeatedly that with a nine-, ten-, or eleven-month-old child, this kind of control, used properly and consistently, will get rid of a bad habit within seven to ten days.

If you have to use this procedure, record the behavior you want to get rid of and the date, and post it somewhere. If the habit is still a part of the baby's behavior after seven to ten days, you are either not restricting your baby's movement enough or for a long enough period of time. I suggest that you lengthen the time after she starts complaining to thirty or even forty-five seconds. Most commonly, the problem resides with the parent's reluctance (understandably) to hold a baby firmly enough because the baby soon begins to cry.

At this point, I have to state something that we have learned that is perhaps the most difficult aspect of the process of raising a secure, unspoiled child. I have never seen the job done well where a baby did not (on occasion) become unhappy because of some restriction put on his behavior by adults. There may be a way to raise a wonderful three-year-old without having to bear up to a baby's crying at times because you set limits on his behavior, but I have never seen it, either in our own education programs or, for that matter, in the many families we have observed at various stages of our research. This is, of course, why, in all my writings since the late 1960s, I have advocated firm, loving control by parents.

The really excellent new information we have learned in recent years is that a firm hand never needs to mean striking a baby. Unfortunately, however, it does mean that parents will occasionally be responsible for their baby's unhappiness as he goes about learning the rules of his family. I should also point out, as I introduce this first form of punishment, that a baby raised with this kind of firm control from seven and one-half months on will invariably become a much happier child as the months go by than another baby whose parents do not exert this kind of control. The happiest two- to three-year-old children have experienced great quantities of love since birth. They have also faced consistent, unwavering limits to certain of their behaviors throughout the seven-and-one-half-to-twenty-two-month period of life.

## 4) Teaching a Child He Has a Limited Right to Insist on Getting His Way or to Repeat Something to Make Sure He Was Understood

This particular goal is the most difficult to achieve. If you fail at it, you'll end up with a child of fourteen months of age who whines and complains a lot and who, in general, is nowhere near as much fun to live with as he might be. Of course, parents don't usually fail at this task completely, nor do they often achieve perfect success. Succeeding involves the same dynamics as preventing bad habits.

Now that your seven-and-one-half- to fourteen-month-old baby has begun to experiment with his newly emerging capacity to insist on getting his way, you need to teach him that there are limits to what he can have. If you ignore this development until a baby is nineteen months old, you will pay dearly. You don't want to prevent a child from learning that he has a right to indicate how much he does or doesn't want something. And, of course, he also should learn that he has a right to make sure you have understood. It is important that he acquire those abilities to communicate with you and to assert himself, but he must also learn that when you set a limit to what he can have or do, you won't back down. He must not be rewarded for throwing a fit or for crying pitifully in the face of your resistance. If those tactics don't get him what he wants, he will stop using them.

Occasionally, by ten to twelve months of age some children will push very hard for something you have refused to give them such as a remote control for a television set or a certain kind of food or snack. The baby may get furious at you and may even start to behave in a way that appears to be potentially self-destructive, such as banging his head against the floor. If that should happen, rest assured that such behavior is "self-limiting." If you don't react to it, it will stop, generally as soon as the baby starts to feel the pain.

## DIAPERING: A GOLDEN OPPORTUNITY

The diapering experience provides an excellent teaching opportunity. When your ten- or eleven-month-old refuses to be diapered, you can either work hard at comforting him, consoling him, or distracting him or you can simply get the job done. I strongly urge you to simply get the job done.

## HOW TO DIAPER A BABY WITH A MINIMUM OF FUSS WHILE AT THE SAME TIME TEACHING HER A VALUABLE LESSON ABOUT LIVING IN HER FAMILY

The first step in the process is being ready. You should always have the needed materials (cleaning items, fresh diapers, and a few small toys for distraction) ready for use. When it it time for a fresh diaper, announce matter-of-factly to the baby that you are going to change her diaper. Do not start to apologize for what you have to do. Take her to the changing table. Give her something to hold and play with. If all is going well, talk to her, have fun. If, on the other hand, she starts to complain or resist by squirming, kicking, and trying to turn over, use your superior strength to get the job done, silently. Do *not* use any more words. Do *not* tell her that you are sorry, that the job will be finished in just a few moments. Unfortunately, this is the classic example of when your concern (the reason you try to explain and console) only reinforces the resistance rather than minimizing it. It is remarkable how universal the resistance is and how much trouble parents get into around this experience.

Your goal should be to teach the baby, from the very beginning of this seven-and-one-half-month period, *total res-*

*ignation* to the inevitability of diapering. You should deal with diapering as you would with inoculations, as something that has to be done, period. In actuality, once understood, diapering becomes an easy and remarkably effective oppportunity for you to teach the baby that you are really in charge and that while she is dearly loved and will most of the time get what she wants, and quickly, sometimes that won't happen. That's just the way things are. Don't forget, however, that if the baby has a bad diaper rash and the cleaning process causes her pain, you need to be more indulgent.

## A SECOND CLASSIC OPPORTUNITY—RESPONDING TO OVERTURES

In *The First Three Years of Life,* when discussing how to help a child acquire first-rate language ability, I described a certain responsive style that we have learned is at the heart of first-rate language development. The behavior is triggered by the normal tendency of the ten- or eleven-month-old infant to approach a parent repeatedly in the regular course of activities. Babies this age, if allowed to, will begin to roam farther and farther away from their parents as they explore the home. Our research indicates that between ten and sixteen months of age a baby will return to a parent and seek contact about ten times an hour. At this tender age, those contacts are for one of three purposes: She may have suffered a bump, in which case she may be whimpering and may need comforting. She may need something like more juice or help with a stuck toy, in which case she may be holding out the empty juice cup or the stubborn toy. Or she may have made an amazing discovery, such as a small, empty box, in which case she may be holding it out for you to marvel over while excitement gleams in her eyes. The effective responsive style we teach consists of the following steps.

1. Respond quickly whenever possible by indicating that you have noticed that she wants your attention.

2. Determine what is on her mind. This is surprisingly easy at this stage of development.

**Here is the important part with respect to the socialization process:**

3. Take a moment to decide whether what your baby wants at that moment is more pressing than what you are doing. Most of the time, you will find that you can interrupt your activity momentarily and attend to her need; these episodes average only twenty-five seconds. If, however, you decide that what you are doing is more important than her need of the moment, say something like, "I hear you, but Mommy's busy now. You'll have to wait."

This simple practice is an example of what we call "healthy selfishness." As with diapering, it is an excellent, frequent opportunity to begin to teach your baby, at a point when it is easiest to teach, that though she is dearly loved and her needs are quite important, they are no more important than those of other people, especially yours.

I realize that you may think such notions are uncaring and not for you. Believe me, if you adopt such a style the benefits will be substantial. The baby will be happy and love you even more.

## SLEEP: A SPECIAL CASE

If you try to initiate naps or bedtime acording to your watch rather than sleep signs, the job is going to be far more difficult than it has to be. Wait until these signs are very clear. That may take five, ten, or more minutes after the first warnings. An exhausted child doesn't complain for very long when it is time for a nap or when it is time to go to bed. Take the child in for a nap and put him in the crib. If the baby is complaining, don't explain anything except to say that it's time for a nap, and then leave. Close the door. If you're using a nursery monitor, do not set the volume on high. If it is set on low, you will hear the loud cries and even the moderate ones. After you've left the room, take a look at your watch and resolve that you're going to wait five full minutes.

If, after five full minutes, the baby is still crying, go into the room, pick him up, bring him out, and let him play again until sleep signs reappear. Once more, wait an additional five to ten minutes or until he can barely keep his eyes open and then try the process again.

This method works most of the time. The idea is to try to avoid the very common practice at this stage of development of teaching the baby that vigorous complaining will quickly get you to do what he wants. A baby has a right to complain, but it must be a limited right. Otherwise, you will be well on the road to a situation where the baby often dictates far more of what's going on in his life than makes any sense at all.

## SETTING LIMITS: THE NEED TO TAKE THE BABY'S POINT OF VIEW INTO ACCOUNT

Parents have no problem setting limits under some circumstances, notably when danger is involved. Picture a twelve-month-old toddler playing in his front yard. Then imagine that the baby's parent looks away for a moment, and the baby begins to move quickly toward the street. The moment the parent sees what is happening, especially if a car happens to be in view, action is immediate. Rushing to the baby and picking her up is, plain and simply, setting a limit. Now change the scene. Think of that same parent trying to change the baby's diaper. The baby resists; she squirms and may even kick. What does the parent do? He tries to distract her. That may or may not work. It certainly won't work for very long. He will very probably keep up a running flow of talk to her, trying to explain that only a few more minutes are needed, etc., while he struggles to finish the job.

What is the baby's point of view in each of these situations? Does the twelve-month-old have any sense that running into the street could have unthinkable consequences? Obviously not. All the baby experiences is her parent suddenly and unequivocally preventing her from doing something she wanted to do. She does not understand the reasons for the differences in her parent's restrictions on her behavior when she tries to run into the street versus the parent's pleading when she resists having her diaper changed. All she can appreciate is that her parent's behavior is inconsistent. To her, the two situations produce mixed messages and confusion.

Such apparent inconsistencies confuse the learning infant and, in turn, make it more difficult for parents to establish a clear message for the baby that there are times when she simply cannot do what she would like—and, further, that those times will be made known to her by clear signals from them. This classic problem helps explain the special usefulness of the diapering experience at this particular period of development.

When an infant (of any age) insists on *anything at all* in spite of your serious opposition, your response should be consistent, regardless of the reasons for your objection. To get through the seven-and-one-half-to-fourteen-month period with the best results, you have to weigh carefully whether you want to set a limit. If you do, you should see to it that the baby abides by that limit. If a baby insists that he drink his grape juice on your new sofa or that he be allowed to touch a sharp knife in the silverware drawer, you should ask yourself whether such a demand is reasonable. Though it may very well be easy for you to go along with that demand, I suggest you don't. Such demands, delivered passionately and insistently by infants, are common during this age period. Here is where our recommendation that you practice "healthy selfishness" becomes relevant. Yielding to these kinds of demands, particularly after you have initially resisted them, undermines your limit-setting authority and, in addition, encourages the baby to satisfy her need at someone else's (your) expense. These are typical learning opportunities of this very special time of life.

During the seven-and-one-half to fourteen-month period, be aware that a baby is learning how to insist on getting her way for the very first time in her life. Teach her that she has that right because she is a dearly loved and valued person. At the same time, however, teach her that her newly acquired right to insist is a limited one, the limit to be set and held to by another dearly lovable and equally valuable person—namely, you. Expect a very large number of explorations of that newly developed talent. As well as you can, examine each demand as it comes along. You'll have no trouble deciding to draw the line when danger is involved, but particularly at this stage of the game, you should try to be firm, *whenever* you decide to draw the line.

What is at stake in setting limits is more than just preventing accidents or tears. Parents who realize that what is involved is whether the baby is learning to accept their authority are more likely to end up with a nicely developing fourteen-month-old than those who are unaware of what really is at stake.

## A MILDER FORM OF LEARNING TO INSIST— INITIATING GAMES

True imitation begins to surface during the last three or four months of the first year of life. Finally, parents begin to have some success teaching a baby to wave bye-bye or to play peek-a-boo or patty-cake. (Many a parent had been trying unsuccessfully for months!) As a baby begins to imitate in this manner, she often is rewarded with dramatic responses from parents and grandparents. Because of the remarkable reinforcing power of the grown-ups' delight, it doesn't take long for such behaviors to become firmly established. Soon thereafter, something new develops, as babies begin to initiate such activities.

Eleven-month-old Caroline had for several weeks been

turning herself around and around while seated on the floor. After a few turns, she would get a little dizzy. Her parents noticed this little habit of hers. They began to throw their arms high and exclaim after Caroline had rotated a few times and started to get woozy. Caroline would then stop, look up at her parents, and glow with pleasure. Within a matter of days, when in the presence of one or both of her parents, Caroline would start to turn herself around, then stop, and without waiting for her parents, throw her arms high and smile with delight while looking at them.

This is one example, of many, of what we call "initiating games." It is the most benign form of using your influence on other people. It is related to the act of insisting on getting your own way and represents another classic sign of a baby's social progress. Please note that it too surfaces in a rather narrow range of time in a baby's life. This is just one more reason I find the social development of a baby during these early years to be such an interesting process.

## SUMMARY

The period of a baby's life from seven and one-half to fourteen months is an extremely important time for guiding a child through early social learning and toward the desired goal of wonderful behavior at three years of age.

At the beginning of this period, the behavior of normal babies is determined by their physical needs for food and comfort, and by their three major interests. Those interests—satisfying curiosity, mastering and enjoying body skills, and socializing with and studying the behavior of the key people in their lives—are each strong and all in balance at seven and one-half months of life. A key task of parents from this point through the first thirty months of life is to provide a world that is rich in developmentally appropriate opportunities and choices the baby can use to nourish each of these primary interests. Habitual confinement at this time of life to playpens, or even small rooms filled with toys, stunts the baby's interests in exploring and mastering her body. In the process, this confinement begins to upset the balance. The common result, especially with a full-time at-home mother and a first baby, is the development of an excessive orientation toward the mother and an overdemanding style on the baby's part. It is not a good idea for either parent to be with the baby on a full-time basis from seven and one-half months on. Getting away from the child for several hours at a stretch, most days, helps to hold down the overdevelopment of the baby's social interest.

Doing a first-rate job of designing a developmentally suitable environment and daily pattern of activities depends on knowledge of the rapidly changing specific interests and abilities of the baby. That information now exists (although it is still imperfect and incomplete) and needs to be learned.

You have to hold down the overdevelopment of the cry as a consequence of common minor mishaps. You also have to be on guard that innocently begun bad habits do not become entrenched. If they do, you should try to remove them as quickly as possible. Finally, the child should be taught that he has a *limited* right to insist on getting what he wants. Also, given his limited ability to communicate, he should be taught that he has the right to repeat his demand *once* in order to be sure that what he wants is understood. However, he must not be taught that if he throws a fit or cries piteously he's going to get what he wants in spite of your initial resistance. Instead, he should learn during this period that he's most often going to get what he wants, and promptly, but that if his parents say what he wants isn't going to happen, that's the end of the story.

The socialization task can be made more difficult, sometimes by factors over which you have no control and at other times by factors you can control. When a baby doesn't start to crawl by seven and one-half or eight months of age or even longer, it becomes more problematic, day by day, to keep the child occupied. Life becomes more difficult for all concerned, and the baby tends to become overly demanding of attention. Situations like this underline the usefulness of walkers and bouncers. Unfortunately, in the case of bouncers, by the time a child gets to be nine and one-half months or ten months of age, he probably will have become too heavy for the apparatus.

Dealing with a late-crawling baby is not easy, but if you follow the principles I described in the preceeding section, chances are you'll do reasonably well. For example, unlike the five-and-one-half- to seven-and-one-half-month-old child, the pre-crawling ten month-old will become very interested in pop-up toys, of which there are quite a number now available. Get them. Use them. By ten months of age or even a little earlier, babies who don't yet crawl will become quite interested in play with board books because of their challenge to the newly developing hand-eye skills. In other words, if you are aware of the developing interests of children during this time, you can compensate somewhat for the lack of rich experiences that come with the ability to crawl and, in the process, hold down the problems that result from the overdevelopment of the social interest.

## SIGNS THAT A NEW STAGE OF SOCIAL DEVELOPMENT IS BEGINNING

The intentional cry for attention at five and one-half to six months and the ability to crawl across a room at seven and one-half to eight months are clear signals that important changes are about to take place in a baby's social development. The picture gets a bit less clear from this point on. I call the next stage of the process "experimenting with power." Some people refer to it as the "no," or "negativistic," stage. It is characterized by the emergence of and fascination with self-consciousness, an awareness for the first time of "me" and "mine." Once your baby really gets into serious explorations of how much power she has in the family, you will know it. The beginning of the stage, however, is not easy to pinpoint, partly because it can start as early as fourteen or as late as eighteen months. Then, too, if your child is an early talker, you may identify the new era when you ask him to give you something and he holds it away from you and says, "no, mine!" In any event, you will know soon enough that your sweet, guileless baby has begun to revel in telling you what to do, after all those months of obediently (for the most part) taking orders from you.

CHAPTER 4

# Fourteen to Twenty-two to Thirty Months*— A Preview of Adolescence

## NORMAL SOCIAL DEVELOPMENT

THE next eight to sixteen months are rich, stressful (no matter how well you do), and vitally important with respect to the social development of your child. Every family we have observed or worked with has had to struggle with their child for at least six months during this period. As the child becomes increasingly aware of his personal power but isn't really sure how much he has, he spends lots of time and energy trying to resolve that unfinished business. At the same time, he continues to be very oriented toward the key people in his life; this is the time he is finalizing his attachment to them. Your major task is to continue to nourish his growing power while at the same time teaching him to respect your rights as well.

*The end of this period varies, depending quite a bit on how parents deal with the dramatic new developments.

# THE DEVELOPMENT OF INTEREST IN PEOPLE

Socially, this period of life is unique with respect to your baby's interest in you. In the preceding period, while she clearly became an avid student of your every reaction to her, the appeal of exploring the home and mastering her body was very powerful. From fourteen months on, however, her interest in your moment-to-moment behaviors will reach an even higher level, one that is not likely to recur at any later time in life.

You may find that your child increasingly sticks to you like glue. The stress that comes from having an eighteen-month-old child no more than five feet away from you, hour after hour, day after day, can be brutal. The reason for this focused behavior is that the fourteen-month-old child has to finish working out a detailed attachment relationship to at least one older person. All normal babies have to go through this process. Creating a social contract with at least one adult is clearly the single most important item of business for the child during the balance of the second year of life (it can and often does continue on into the third year as well). Once that basic necessity is taken care of, the child will turn much of her social energy toward learning to relate to peers.

Throughout this period, you should expect your baby to show some wariness about most other adults. While the typical toddler (fourteen to twenty-four months) tends to stay quite near his parents when out of his home, about one in five do not show the usual signs of caution during this age range. Such children tend to be friendly toward most adults. No one knows why such differences exist among children.

## The Social Basis for the Appeal of Balls and Books

The single most played-with object during the four-teen-to-twenty-two-month period of life is a ball. Babies of this age love all kinds of balls, big or little, firm or squishy. Probably the best value of any toy you could buy is a two-dollar, large (twenty-four-inch) plastic beach ball. Why do toddlers love balls? I think there are three reasons. As Piaget has reported, babies show great interest in the movements of objects from the time they are seven months old and start dropping food from their high chairs (curiosity). Then, too, a ball is an appropriate object with which to practice throwing and retrieving (the motor interest). The third special usefulness of balls, however, is that they lend themselves to fun play with (and showing off to) one's parents (the social interest).

During this stage of life, when babies concentrate on coming to terms with their parents, any toy or other object that can be used with a parent has special appeal. The same is true, of course, when it comes to books. The way in which books bring your baby and you close makes it easy to establish a book habit in children during the first two years of life. At fourteen months of age, if books have been available most babies have already developed an interest in them. At that stage, their interest in gumming them has lessened, as has the challenge of separating and turning the pages (the motor interest). What is growing is the baby's interest in the contents of the book (curiosity), and especially her interest in being close to you (the social interest) with the book. Closeness to you and your undivided attention mean more and more as the days go by. Gradually, a book session becomes an arena for experimenting with power as well.

## Do Babies This Age Need to Spend Time with Other Toddlers?

A good many parents nowadays think, for one reason or another, that this is an age when babies should play well with one another. Indeed, many people think that children need regular exposure to children their own age during this time. I do not believe that is true at all. For one thing, it is very clear that many normal children of this age are capable of significant physical aggression toward other children of similar age. I have watched many situations where an eighteen-month-old, using strictly physical tactics, quickly began to intimidate a second baby. In the process, the dominant child began to develop into a bully, while the other became increasingly submissive. People who work regularly with groups of toddlers are well aware of this problem. I can't think of a single benefit of this kind of experience for either child. Unfortunately, similar dynamics operate in the case of closely spaced siblings (see below).

You should also be aware that you must be responsible every moment for your own child's social behavior when he is in the company of another child who is close in age. While you can expect wonderful, civil enjoyment when your eighteen-month-old interacts with your neighbor's four- or five-year-old, that simply is not at all likely if your eighteen-month-old is interacting with another child who is sixteen to twenty-four months of age.

### The Toddler's Creed

If I want it, it's mine.

If I give it to you and change my mind later, it's mine.

If I can take it away from you, it's mine.

If I had it a little while ago, it's mine.

If it's mine, it will never belong to anyone else, no matter what.

If we are building something together, all the pieces are mine.

If it looks like mine, it's mine.

On occasion I have seen remarkably advanced eighteen- to twenty-month-olds interacting maturely with others similar in age. It is not that it can't happen; it is just that you must not expect it. Interacting in a civil manner means no physical aggression whatsoever. It means some true interest in what the other child is doing, and it also means being able to take turns well. It means being willing to share toys and other materials. Such behavior is quite rare in this age range.

Whereas the seven-and-one-half- to fourteen-month-old baby has identified the key people in her life, and needs to know a lot more about their reactions to her various behaviors, now the message of the baby's behavior becomes more complicated and intense. It's as if the baby is saying, "I need these people, especially when I'm not at home, and I need them even more than I did before. They are my security. I like older children a lot, especially four- and five-year-olds, and I like looking at tiny babies; they're cute and unthreatening. I also like looking at puppies, cats, and squirrels. Babies my own age, however, are quite another story. I am learning that there will be a fair amount of trouble if I spend much time with them."*

## Sibling Rivalry

It is impossible to do a proper job of describing social development during the early years without discussing the effects of sibling rivalry. They simply have far too much potency to be ignored. Parents are often embarrassed to admit that their children fight with each other. If you ask a parent how her three-year-old likes his eighteen-month-old brother, you might hear the following kind of answer. "Oh, he really loves his baby brother. They play together so well! There are times, of course, when he doesn't seem to know his own strength, but he does love him." In our home observations of such pairs, we almost invariably find that three-

---

*Let me remind the reader that during the first two years of life babies are capable of only limited thinking at best. When I use this kind of method to describe what seem to be the themes that underlie their social behaviors, I not mean in any way to suggest that babies actually think about these notions.

year-olds do *not* love their eighteen-month-old siblings much of the time. On the contrary, such pairs fight a lot, hour after hour, day after day. Any parent at home full-time has her hands full.

The kind of impact sibling rivalry has on the child's social development depends on the ages of the other siblings. In the earlier discussion of the seven-and-one-half-to-fourteen-month period, I pointed out that daily life could become quite problematic and trying for a baby with a sibling less than three years older. During the fourteen-to-twenty-four-month period, as the child's interpersonal strength and power grow appreciably, he becomes less willing to be exclusively on the receiving end of abuse from his older sibling. Indeed, younger children who are particularly feisty begin to become initiators of squabbles with their older siblings during this time of life. This is when biting and hair pulling come into the baby's repertoire. They are superb weapons against someone who is older and stronger. It generally takes a while for parents to come to the depressing realization that when they hear fighting between the children they can no longer be sure that the older one started it.

A younger child can come to dominate a slightly older child at this time. After all, the older child has had much more experience with pain, so she quickly learns to be fearful about being bitten or having her hair pulled. Furthermore, her hostile acts aimed at the baby have been forbidden by her parents. On top of all that, the baby observes no rules of fair combat.

Another possibility as a child approaches two is for him to have a newly crawling younger sibling in his life. All it takes is a twelve-to fourteen-month gap between children. The twenty-two- to twenty-four-month-old child who has been concentrating intensely on interrelations with his mother now finds that process of major importance interrupted increasingly as the younger child becomes a crawler and a climber. The principal effect of these circumstances is that the older child becomes more and more irritated and begins to feel jealous and unhappy.

Another possibility, of course, is for a baby between twenty-two and twenty-four months to be sandwiched between a slightly older *and* a newly crawling sibling. Middle babies are less predictable. Usually the closely spaced second child is more aggressive than an only child because she has had to learn to defend herself against her jealous older sibling. On the other hand, unlike her older sibling, she never was the only child in the home, and therefore her displacement by the new baby is less than what her older sibling experienced.

The effect of a child's birth order on his social development is not always clear, but one thing is very clear. Close spacing of children always makes the child-raising task much more difficult. It is also clear that an overindulged older child always has a harder time with the problems of sibling rivalry.

## THE DEVELOPMENT OF SPECIAL SOCIAL ABILITIES

During the period from fourteen to twenty-two to thirty months, children hone each of the five special social abilities that began to develop during the first fourteen months. Toddlers become remarkably savvy about anticipating the array of responses their parents will show to their behavior. The twenty-four-month-old clearly knows exactly which buttons to push.

The ability to gain attention in socially acceptable ways may move ahead steadily or progress may be less impressive, but usually the two-year-old is considerably more talented than a fourteen-month-old in this respect.

The normal new achievements of this period can lead

to a steady increase in a baby's sense of pride in herself. The outcome of this important process depends directly on how much time a baby spends with her key people. Under most circumstances, no one can nurture this particular development as effectively as parents and grandparents.

Expressing feelings toward an older person likewise can become more complex and more appropriate or it may be stifled, depending on the reactions of the key people to the baby's behavior. If, for example, a baby lives with a harried mother who has several other children and an altogether unhappy life, he may find that tolerance for free expression of his feelings (especially his anger) is limited. Certainly during these ten months a child has ample time to learn through thousands of episodes what is and what isn't accepted in his own family. We have seen a fair number of two-year-olds who have learned to fear their own mother. And we have seen this even though we have never performed research in seriously troubled homes. (It is far more common, however, for a child to learn to fear an older sibling or to dislike a younger one during this period.)

Make-believe or pretend play that surfaces shortly after the first birthday usually has an altogether delightful quality to it. It is the kind of behavior that parents naturally tend to reinforce, and should reinforce. As the child approaches the end of the fourteen-to-twenty-two-to-thirty-month period, the emergence of considerably greater language ability and higher mental ability will enable him to really appreciate stories. A playful attitude on your part and some enthusiasm about your baby's make-believe activities and stories appear to be major factors that encourage this kind of imaginative play. Clearly a child who is left on his own most of the time won't receive that kind of encouragement.

•  •  •

# THE DEVELOPMENT OF A SOCIAL STYLE

## From Initiating Games to Directing Activities

Directing behavior becomes very well developed during the fourteen-to-twenty-two-month period. It had its roots in the tendency of the ten- to eleven-month-old to initiate games with his parents. Having learned (via imitation) to respond to patty-cake and peek-a-boo between nine and ten months of age, the child experiences a turnaround in which, at ten to eleven months, he begins to initiate such activities in order to get a previously appreciated response from a parent. Initiating games evolves into directing parents and, in turn, in the third year of life, into leadership skill with peers.

One consequence of the exhilaration that comes with the first awareness that they have some degree of power over the big folks who run their lives is that babies begin to take huge delight in telling their parents what to do. This often surfaces at playtime, with the willing parent, often the father, waiting on his child hand and foot. It is a game that everybody enjoys. For example, you may suggest that your daughter bring you one of her books. Most fourteen-month-olds really like that request. You may suggest that she choose from among a few. At first, she probably won't have clear favorites, but over the next few months you can expect them to appear. You can't help but notice that she enjoys being given the opportunity to choose. As the weeks go by, you will find she enjoys the act of choosing more and more. Gradually, she will become more assertive. Soon she will not only get the book on her own, she will make it clear that she wants you to read it to her. She will probably develop the habit of backing into your lap. Sooner or later, usually by sixteen or seventeen months, you will find that she will want to dictate the rate at which you turn the pages. Don't be surprised if she insists on turning the page before you have finished reading it. It will be obvious at times that she has become more interested in "directing" you than in listening to you read. This, of course, is different from the other times when she will get a book, sit down with it, and "read" it by herself. That kind of solitary activity is motivated by curiosity. Directing you in a book session is, for the most part, a social affair.

At other times, there will be a game that everybody is used to playing and that had been initiated by one of the parents in the past, but that the child now seeks to initiate over and over and over again.

Elizabeth, a nineteen-month-old, was delighted to be introduced by her parents to a new circle game called Round and Round the Mulberry Bush, the Monkey Chased the Weasel. At the place in the song where the words are "and they all fall down," everyone does. In this group participation game, everybody ends up slightly dizzy and falling down a lot. For most adults, two or three times around the bush is enough.

Elizabeth fell in love with this game immediately. After two or three rounds, something changed. Instead of waiting for her mother or father to suggest they do it again, Elizabeth began to shout "Bush, bush!" She wanted more. At first, they were delighted at their child's enjoyment in the game and in her newfound executive ability. Unfortunately, Elizabeth wasn't happy with one, two, or even three more times around the mulberry bush. Like most children her age, she was into repetition. Day in and day out, this twenty-three-inch-tall toddler kept demanding that her parents play the game with her. She sometimes would include her dolls in the game, but the most important participants were her parents. After a while, her mother begged off, but only with the promise that her father would continue to play. That he did, under some duress, for many additional days.

This budding executive ability in the fourteen-to-twenty-two-month period works best with parents and grandparents. When one eighteen-month-old tries it on another eighteen-month-old, the practice can lead to grief. Parents and grandparents, however, usually enjoy it immensely (at least the first twenty times).

Sometimes this "directing" activity evolves into mildly tyrannical behavior by the second year of life. On the other hand, it can develop into a healthy kind of "taking turns" behavior. In either case, it will express itself in play with peers during the third year of life.

## THE BALANCE AMONG THE PRIMARY INTERESTS

Because of the extraordinarily strong social needs of the child during this stage of life, it is easy for the balance among the primary interests to be lost to some degree. If a parent is overprotective and tends to sharply limit a toddler's natural interest in climbing, that tends to lessen the motor interest. If a baby lives in a home where he is kept confined to one room or other limited space, curiosity starts to be inhibited. If a parent is with the child nearly all the time, the tendency for overattachment is increased at the expense of the other major interests. Whether the balance is maintained depends directly on the child-rearing practices adopted by the family. The balance is easily and commonly disturbed. It need not be.

## THE COMPLAINING/HAPPINESS INDEX

When a child develops poorly during this period, you can expect that his day will feature lots of complaining and testing of his parents' authority. When the process has gone well, complaining will be minimal (though not nonexistent), and best of all, the child will seem happy most of the time. Complaining will occur, of course, but at a lower level, and it will begin to recede substantially at about nineteen months. These simple features are reliable indicators of the impact of various child-rearing practices.

In my judgment, this is a remarkably important time of life with respect to social development. What parents do in this and the preceding period (seven and one-half to fourteen months) has major significance in shaping the personality of each new child. The fourteen-to-twenty-four-month period of life is almost always the most difficult of the first three years for all parents, including those whose children are developing well. For children who are not developing terribly well, the third year can be even more difficult. It is a time when parents put the finishing touches on a child's basic personality. They have this power, whether they realize it or not.

During the seven-and-one-half-to-fourteen-month period, the central focus in a child's social life is on the careful examination of all the noticeable effects of her behaviors on the primary adults in her life. From fourteen months through twenty-two to thirty months of age, that central focus changes. Now the phrase that best describes the burning purpose of a normal child in her social interactions becomes "experimentation with power." The key activity that helps her determine (with exquisite precision) just how much power she has in each of the numerous circumstances of her life is the process of "testing." If you can distance the often difficult emotions that are involved, it is an extremely interesting process. Of course, if you're living in the situation, distancing the emotions is virtually impossible. In all probability, I appreciate this process more than the parents we work with do.

I will never forget an early observtion when Charles, an agile nineteen-month-old, took a quick look at his mother to be sure that she was watching him, and then moved quickly out of the kitchen and into the living room. As he went, he looked back two or three times to see if his mother was still watching him. Satisfied that she was, he raced to the coffee table, climbed onto it, turned around to face her as she approached, and jumped up and down on the table repeatedly, while looking toward her to see the effect. You might consider this kind of behavior to reflect some sort of genetic malformation. Not at all! This kind of behavior is quite typical of children from sixteen or seventeen through thirty months of age.

A new, exciting development that ushers in the active pursuit of information about children's interpersonal power is the emergence of an awareness of self, which begins to surface between fourteen and sixteen months of age. We are indebted to Piaget's work for this information. It is easy to confirm the existence of this new advance in mental activity in children who begin to talk earlier than most. Two unmistakable signs indicate that the sense of self has surfaced. The first is the use of the possessive pronoun, often following the word "no" as in, "No, mine" when, for example, the fifteen-month-old is asked to give something to another person. The second is the use of the possessive form of one's name following the word "no," as in, "No, Shirley's." While there may be some subtle, technical reason for denying that these utterances reflect a sense of self, they're convincing enough for me.

A central goal of the naturalistic observations we did in homes starting in the late 1960s was to identify all the different tasks children engage in during their daily lives. We coined the phrase "to assert self" to describe behaviors that surfaced at around one year of age. Typically, the label was applied to episodes where a baby refused a request or an order from his parent. Such behavior seemed to represent the flexing of newly found interpersonal muscles.

Another term often used to describe these new developments is "negativism." An infant who has entered the negativistic state begins to show a growing tendency to behave in an ornery fashion. The sense of self, the tendency to assert oneself, and negativism are all intertwined. Full-blown negativism is quite dramatic to behold. The child in such a state seems to have become drunk with power. A baby in such a state will often be so dedicated to opposing his parents that he will turn down a suggestion that is usually very attractive to him in order to make it clear just who is *boss* of the situation.

The beginnings of negativism or asserting oneself can be seen in some children as early as fourteen months, a month or two earlier in some, or as late as eighteen or nineteen months in others. They most commonly begin to be obvious between fifteen and sixteen months of age. Of course, babies may show "previews of coming attractions" toward the end of the first year. Once this tendency to stubbornly refuse to go along with parents' ordinary, simple requests surfaces, it grows fairly steadily over the next six months or so. For some children, negativism continues to be a major feature of their social interactions well into their third year. (Indeed, for some it persists for years!) Ordinarily, this negativism gets to the point where it reveals both a very impressive degree of determination on the part of the child and a clearly subrational quality. When we ask any parent of a twenty-month-old whether the child engages in any behavior that indicates that she has a strong will, the answer, generally preceded by a gasp and expressed with great emphasis, is, "Does she ever!"

In the chronic difficulty that parents have with children in the heat of negativism and testing—and in the clearly subrational nature of their objections—the similarity to adolescent behavior becomes clear. As far as we can tell, no parent goes through this period of a baby's life with ease. This is definitely not the time to engage in needless hassling with a child—for example, pushing hard to get toilet training accomplished.

This is a time when psychological testing of children is rarely feasible. Most tests, after all, consist of a series of simple requests to children, such as "Can you show me where the cat is?" or "Can you draw a circle?" Many a nineteen-or-twenty-month-old certainly can do these things but is not about to. You're often better off if you say, "I know you don't know where a cat is, so let's go on to the next page." What often follows is that, with a coy smile, a twenty-month-old may very well jump at the opportunity to demonstrate that you are wrong.

## THE MANY SOCIAL LESSONS TODDLERS LEARN

The fourteen-to-twenty-four-month period of a child's life is both exciting and stressful for all concerned. Everyone hopes the child will emerge from subrationality and testing by twenty-two to twenty-four months of age. If that happens, the result is almost too wonderful to describe, and I am not exaggerating. Children do not, unfortunately, come with guarantees. To a substantial extent, their development is a do-it-yourself affair. Many a two-year-old has clearly become spoiled. You may be reading this book because you know such a child and are resolved not to have your child develop in the same way.

During this especially formative period in a child's life, he will continue to learn just how valuable he is in his family. He will learn whether his needs are routinely met or not. He will learn a huge amount about the key people in his life, especially as it relates to power. He will learn about these themes, to some degree, separately for each important adult in his life—his mother, his father, and any other adult he spends a good deal of time with. For most children, the learning in respect to their mothers is the most important and will remain so well into the third year. Increasingly during this stage, if the father is an active participant, he acquires a good deal of significance. Whether he ever reaches equity with a child's mother is not fully understood.

• • •

# WHEN THINGS GO WRONG

There is absolutely no question in my mind that the most difficult developmental period for both parents and children when the process is going well is the fourteen-to-twenty-two- to twenty-four-month period. When things are going badly, the difficult period is prolonged. Usually the worst is over by thirty months, but many a child who has been grossly overindulged during his first thirty months of life continues to be a chronic source of stress and unhappiness in the family for a long time thereafter.

At the same time that parents are trying to cope with an increasingly rebellious, subrational toddler, they also have to be on guard against the continued possibility of serious damage from falls from high places and accidental poisonings. Mercifully, as the baby approaches two years of age, the likelihood of such accidents declines substantially. Unmercifully, with each month that passes after that, the spoiled child becomes more and more of a terror.

If a baby reaches fourteen months of age having become a successful whiner, the prospects for the next ten to sixteen months are nowhere near as bright as they otherwise would have been. In the weeks that follow fourteen months, negativism and self-assertion emerge rapidly and take on a more combative and intense quality in such a child than they do with the well-developing child of the same age. The other classic sign that the struggle has really begun is "testing" behavior.

A year or so ago, I was conducting a home visit with two parents and their twenty-one-month-old child. At that age, most children require the attention of their parents every few minutes (if their parents are nearby). At twenty-one months of age, children who have been chronically overindulged require even more of their parents' attention. They especially do not enjoy a situation where their parent is engaged in conversation with another person. Well, Henry certainly didn't like the situation. After about ten to twelve minutes during which he felt he wasn't being sufficiently attended to, Henry started to cross the living room, all the while fixing his father with a stare. He moved about twelve feet toward a tall floor plant. It was a lovely plant, of which both parents were quite fond. As the child approached the plant, he put his right arm out and reached in its direction. His father's gaze was now totally fixed on him, his expression serious. Henry got to the plant and slowly and deliberately squeezed a leaf between his thumb and his index finger. He didn't pull it off. He simply squeezed it. In a split second, his father burst out with "No! Henry!" Just as quickly, Henry's face lit up with a big smile. It was painfully obvious that this wasn't the first time Henry had threatened that plant. Indeed, it was probably at least the fiftieth time. Henry knew his father like a book that he had memorized perfectly.

Henry's well-practiced behavior very clearly illustrates several aspects of his development. Obviously, Henry had developed a large appetite for his parents' attention. Compared with that of a well-developed child his age, his need was clearly excessive and typical of an overindulged twenty-one-month-old. Just as obviously, he knew that if he engaged in certain previously forbidden actions, he could count on getting the attention he craved and getting it promptly. The behavior also illustrates very clearly his father's inability to control his son. In this case, Henry's mother was even less effective than his father, making the matter even more problematic than usual.

Let me hastily assure you that even if you've done an absolutely perfect job with your child for the first fourteen months, you still are going to have to put up with a minimum of six months of the child testing and in other ways "experimenting with interpersonal power." It seems that this difficult process is simply a requirement in early human development, or at least it is with respect to the wide variety of families that we have studied. What that means is that there is no way to avoid a fair amount of stress in the socialization process during the fourteen-to-twenty-two-month period. It is clear, however, that one can either keep this inevitable period of stress to a six- to eight-month span or subject oneself and one's child to a considerably longer and much more intensive struggle. The inevitability of substantial stress during these months is why we do not recommend full-time parenting for anyone during a child's second year of life.

## The Emergence of the Capacity to Bully

During the fourteen-to-twenty-four-month period, especially as the child moves toward the end of the second year of life, overindulged children who have not been taught to respect the rights of their parents commonly begin to develop a tyrannical or bullying style.

Sonya was developing beautifully. Almost everything had gone well throughout the first eighteen months of her life, with the exception of sleep. The child often complained about naps, and her mother wasn't altogether happy about that situation. On the whole, this didn't happen so often that it was considered a serious problem. It seemed to us, however, to reflect the tendency on the child's part to throw her weight around a bit too much. She would cry rather forcefully at times when she was put down for a nap. We were able to help the mother cope with that problem, but it wasn't easy.

Sonya's mother had been using a nursery monitor with the volume set high. That meant the child's complaints boomed into her mother's ears. We got Sonya's mother to lower the volume on the monitor, take a look at her watch, and brace herself for five minutes from the time Sonya started hard crying. After three minutes, which to her mother would have felt like ten if she hadn't used her watch, Sonya went to sleep. So far, so good.

In the weeks that followed, however, Sonya started getting up at two or three in the morning and refusing to go

**Interpersonal Development**   14 months to 22–30 months

*Age in months*   14   16   17   18   20   22   24   26   28   30

CATEGORIES

*Direction of Social Interest*
Key Adults Only
• Stranger anxiety
• Separation anxiety
Slightly Older Siblings
Younger Siblings (at least 8 months of age)
Peers

*Social Competencies*
Getting attention using intentional cry
Getting attention (other means)
Using adults as a resource

176

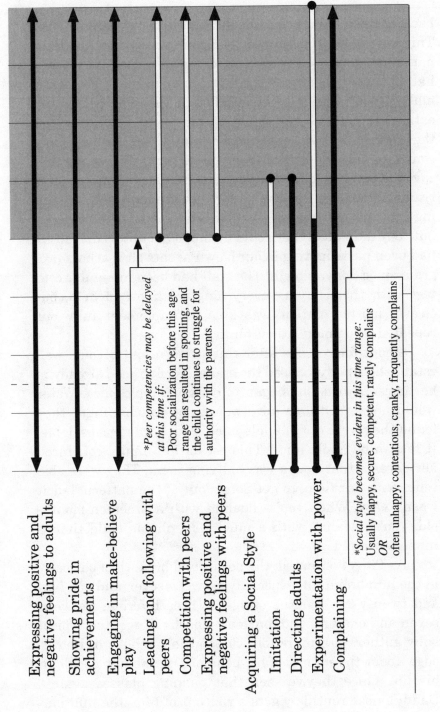

Expressing positive and negative feelings to adults

Showing pride in achievements

Engaging in make-believe play

Leading and following with peers

Competition with peers

Expressing positive and negative feelings with peers

Acquiring a Social Style

Imitation

Directing adults

Experimentation with power

Complaining

*Peer competencies may be delayed at this time if:
Poor socialization before this age range has resulted in spoiling, and the child continues to struggle for authority with the parents.

*Social style becomes evident in this time range:
Usually happy, secure, competent, rarely complains
OR
often unhappy, contentious, cranky, frequently complains

LEGEND:

Range of onset or termination

Duration

back to sleep unless she was allowed into her parents' bed. This kind of sleep disturbance in children who for the most part have done well with sleep during the first year and a half of their lives is not at all uncommon, but that doesn't make it any easier to bear. Though she was petite and extremely cute, Sonya would become very demanding on these occasions. No explanation would work. She simply would scream for half an hour or longer until her parents caved in and brought her into their bed. She began a regular ritual of getting up at two or three in the morning, screaming until she got what she wanted. Her parents didn't like it, but they didn't feel they could do much about it. This family had been participating in our New Parents as Teachers program since Sonya's birth. The staff had been in regular contact with them, trying everything we knew to help, but clearly neither parent was able to implement fully our repeated recommendations for firmness.

About four weeks after this pattern had become well established, Sonya raised the stakes. At five A.M., already in her parents' bed, she began to demand apple juice. Water would not do. Orange juice would not do. One night they found they were out of apple juice. Sonya was inconsolable. It had to be apple juice. This escalation finally convinced her parents that Sonya was bullying them. They were able then, with our help, to get Sonya out of the pattern, but it wasn't easy. When you're dealing with a nineteen-month-old, you're dealing with a much less pliable child than a nine-month-old.

As Piaget observed, the power and breadth of curiosity in the human infant, especially between seven and one-half and twenty-two months of age, is breathtaking. Between seven and one-half and fourteen months of age, the typical baby gathers a remarkably substantial amount of knowledge about the impact of his behavior on the key people in his life. Once they've seen that pushing glasses against Daddy's nose routinely gets a rise out of him, the information gets stored. When they have seen that "dancing" to music regularly gets their parents to make a big fuss over them, they store that information, too. They begin to know their parents and their reactions to many of their behaviors in a manner that parallels the knowledge that parents gain about how to comfort their baby during the first three to four months of his life.

The child who skillfully uses the whine at thirteen or fourteen months has learned that whining frequently gets him what he wants. He is well launched on a course of social development that becomes extremely difficult for all concerned during the very special period from fourteen to twenty-two to thirty months of life.

## THREE MAJOR CONSEQUENCES OF POOR SOCIALIZATION DURING THE SEVEN-AND-ONE-HALF-TO-TWENTY-TWO-MONTH PERIOD

If a child becomes a spoiled two-year-old, several substantial problems will result. The first is that the child simply won't be anywhere near as enjoyable a person to have in the family as he could have been.

The second consequence is that not only will he be overly self-centered and demanding, but he won't be as happy as he otherwise might have been. He will have become a chronic complainer. Of course, there will be times when he will seem contented, especially when he is the center of attention. All too frequently, however, he will be overly demanding, impatient, inclined to taunt you, and in general not much fun to be with. Any parent at home full-time with such a child will be living with a substantial amount of daily stress. In contrast, unspoiled two-year-olds are usually deliriously happy most of the time. From the time he wakes up in the morning until he goes to bed at night, the nicely developing two-year-old is a joy to live with. Believe me, it's true.

The third problem has to do with the shift of social

focus from parents to peers. Until a child has stopped struggling with his parents for authority, that child is a poor prospect for making friends with children his own age. Who wants to play with someone who cries a lot, hits, won't share, and is dissatisfied much of the time? If by twenty-four months of age a child has not learned to respect his parents' authority, the struggle invariably gets worse during the months that follow.

When social development goes well during the first two years of life, the child, having come to terms with his parents, will begin to explore the world of peers in a truly social way. Babies are interested in agemates when they are younger, of course, but for the most part, that interest is similar to the kind of interest they would show in a turtle: genuine, but not very social.

## HOW TO GUIDE YOUR CHILD THROUGH THE MOST DIFFICULT STAGE OF SOCIAL DEVELOPMENT— FOURTEEN TO TWENTY-TWO MONTHS

With good luck and effective parenting, you now have a fourteen-month-old child who is not only gorgeous but is usually great fun to be with. Not only have such well-behaved fourteen-month-old children learned to accept the authority of their parents, but they are obviously much happier than those who have been overindulged. There is an undeniable difference between a family situation where the fourteen-month-old has developed into a small tyrant and a situation where the child has really learned that when his mother says "no" that's pretty much it. In the latter case, a child may occasionally test her parents' authority, but such occasions will be few and far between.

I've been in several homes where fourteen-month-old children, who had been chronically overindulged, consistently made life miserable for everybody—not only for their parents and visitors, but for themselves as well. They had acquired very little ability to cope with frustration, as evidenced by the way their complaints quickly escalated to screams and then to loud crying accompanied by full flowing tears. Surely no baby enjoys behaving like that, and I am convinced that such a condition need not have developed. If, like my co-workers and me, you had the privilege of observing hundreds of children, on a month-to-month schedule, I don't have the slightest doubt that you would see how overindulgence of a baby leads to this kind of unhappy situation. You don't have to be a genius or even terribly clever to identify major differences in parenting styles and to link them consistently to contrasting social developments in babies.

## THE GOAL—THE BENEFITS OF RAISING AN ABSOLUTELY WONDERFUL, HAPPY, SECURE, AND SOCIALLY EFFECTIVE TWENTY-TWO-MONTH-OLD CHILD

You may wonder why I set the goal at twenty-two months of age. Over the last twenty-five years or so, we have watched a large number of families raise their babies. Babies usually start testing the parents' authority seriously by about sixteen months of age. We have never seen a family get away with less than six months of struggling over these issues. When a family has managed to pull out of the problem stage by twenty-two months of age, they enter into an absolutely heavenly new phase. If they're not quite out of the woods but buckle down and finish the job by the time the child is two years old, we think they've done wonderfully well indeed—perhaps nine on a scale of ten. If by two years of age they are still struggling with the child, if the child is still not trustworthy when they take him out to a restaurant or a mall, if the child repeatedly seeks out situations where he can test the parents, then the parents are in trouble. If by twenty-six to twenty-eight months of age that condition still exists, then they've got their hands full. In the months that follow, they're very likely to have a child who will engage in what we call "terrible twos" behavior, throwing tantrums, particularly in public places, and all in all taking a lot of joy out of being a parent—and, for that matter, of being a child.

As revealed in Piaget's classic work, the ability to think—to engage in higher mental processes involving the manipulation of ideas, reflection, the weighing of alternatives and making judgments—surfaces in human beings somewhere between a year and one-half to two years of age. Interestingly, one very clear sign of this new and exciting ability is the appearance of the first lies.

In our video series, twenty-three-month-old Tina is kneeling on a chair at the kitchen table between her parents. She is a bright child, and she dearly loves attention. There is milk in a mug in front of her and doughnuts on the table nearby. The family is having a pleasant little interchange, and Tina is showing off, something she tends to do a lot. Throughout her short life, Tina has been surrounded by an extended family and by many others who have told her how great she is (many times). To maintain the spotlight, Tina reaches for a spoon and a knife and holds them high above her head while looking at her mother (for her reaction). Her mother, having had enough of the situation, says, "All right, Tina, give me those. I want to put them in the sink." Tina looks at her and says, "No, Tina's," thereby revealing, in a classic fashion, her self-conscious use of her personal power to assert her rights against those of her mother. (Of course it is also an example of her negativism.) Her mother then reaches in the general direction of Tina and the silverware. Tina tries to avoid her and in the process tips the mug of milk over on the table, flooding a fairly large area and soaking several doughnuts. Her mother says, "Oh" (unhappily) and immediately gets a paper towel and starts to sop up the milk. Tina, still kneeling on the chair, hangs her head and watches the proceedings. After about five seconds, her father says to her, "Good show, kid, you're all right." Five seconds later he says (with mock seriousness), "Who did that? Did Tina do that?" Another five seconds elapse and Tina, her head still facing down in a posture of guilt, says in a quiet voice and with a straight face, "I didn't do it, Lisa [her older sister] did it." Clearly, in order to create such an answer the gears had to turn in this twenty-three-month-old's head. This is only one of many ways in which children show that they are thinking creatures even before they are two years old.

Parallel to this new capacity to create original ideas (in this case to think up a lie to avoid taking responsibility for a punishable act), the normal twenty-three-month-old child has usually come a long way when it comes to verbal expression. Though there are exceptions even among well-developing children, the vast majority become talking machines just before they turn two.

Look, then, at what joy you'll have coming to you if you do a nice job of socializing your child during the first twenty-two months. You will have a child who will be reasonable. You will have a child who will be thoughtful at times. You will have a child who will come out with original notions and will be able to express them to you reasonably well. You'll have a child with whom you can converse. You will have a child who regularly reveals that she has a sense of humor. You will be positively amazed at how much is going on inside your child's head.

This, then, is part of your reward for having done a first-rate job. It is part of what you get for having had the determination and willingness to let your child cry once in a while during the seven-and-one-half-to-twenty-two-month period, when you felt it necessary to set limits.

Another very important consequence of achieving this goal by twenty-two months of age is that a nicely developed twenty-two-month-old will be ready to begin forming friendships with his peers. Eighteen- and nineteen-month-old children get a huge amount of enjoyment out of interactions with four-, five-, and six-year-olds. They're even nice to babies, although they don't stay with them for very long. Put that same child together with a peer, give or take a month or two, and you get very different results. Eighteen-month-old children do not often treat each other nicely. Occasionally, you'll get two very well-behaved, very mature, very quiet and nonaggressive eighteen-month-olds who will play well together. This is definitely the exception, not the rule.

The twenty-four-month-old who has been regularly overindulged is not very interested in forming friendships with other children. In addition, other children will not enjoy his company. By way of contrast, the twenty-two-month-old who has been socialized well will relate quite nicely to peers who are equally well developed and, of course, to older children as well.

Another important reason to work very hard to attain this goal is if another baby is either already in the family or on the way. When children are spaced closer than three years apart, sibling rivalry becomes the single most difficult phenomenon parents have to cope with. The difficulties begin when the younger child becomes a crawler at roughly seven and one-half months of age. The spoiled two-year-old is a holy terror with an eight- or nine-month-old competitor. I must say that even the beautifully developed twenty-two-month-old does not generally find such unfair competition attractive.

These, then, are some of the reasons for dedicating yourself to doing a first-rate job of avoiding spoiling during the fourteen-to-twenty-four-month period of your child's life. Take advantage of this very special opportunity to put the finishing touches on your child's rapidly crystallizing personality. Remember, the vast majority of parents are capable of doing this job well.

· · · ·

# HOW TO RAISE AN ABSOLUTELY WONDERFUL TWENTY-TWO-MONTH-OLD CHILD

The following recommendations will work. They will work best when both parents are familiar with them and cooperate fully with each other. You will need determination and energy and perseverance. Remember, these next eight to ten months are quite special. Your direct impact in shaping your child's personality peaks during this very brief time of her life.

Being able to exercise her budding authority becomes increasingly important to the child in the fourteen-to-twenty-four-month period. Parents, therefore, should provide opportunities for her to exercise this new ability in socially acceptable ways, but within limits. For example, often eighteen-or nineteen-month-old children will start to become very choosy about the clothes they're going to wear. If you anticipate that your child will enjoy telling you just what he'll allow you to put on him, you can bring out two or three shirts or pairs of socks and give him his choice. Don't be surprised if he rejects all three and continues to reject subsequent offerings. The opportunity to control a parent's behavior at this stage of development means far more to a child than the color of his socks. As a result, many a parent of a twenty-month-old finds herself spending fifteen to twenty minutes getting him dressed, not realizing that what the child is interested in is power, not fashion.

## Experimenting with Power

If limit setting has gone well and the twelve-month-old is learning that he has the right to insist on getting his own way, but that his parents will, at times, firmly set a limit to that right, the process begins to take a somewhat different path. Such a child will continue to increase the frequency of testing behvior but almost always in the pursuit of learning what will and what won't be allowed, rather than how to force attention. He really isn't sure of what his parents will do when he wanders into another room or begins to explore a dish towel or the vacuum cleaner. He needs to learn about how each parent reacts to large numbers of acts and situations he engages in day by day.

As he moves into the fourteen-to-sixteen-month period, the purpose of his testing behavior changes in a very important way. It is no longer a question of not being sure of your reactions. That stage is behind him. Now he is using what he is certain you disapprove of to learn just how much power he has. In other words, no matter how good a job you are doing, you cannot totally avoid coping with some testing as your child experiments with power. That is why we sometimes refer to the fourteen-to-twenty-two-month period as a "preview of adolescence."

If all is going well, your baby will begin to do less testing during his twentieth month. If you have done a superb job, testing will, for the most part, disappear by the time your baby is twenty-two months old. If it stops by twenty-four months of age, you have done wonderfully well.

When the process is not going well, not only does testing not diminish during the twentieth month of life, it continues to increase. That is not a good sign. In such cases, testing begins to aquire a new and quite unpleasant tone. It becomes tormenting. The overindulged two- to three-year-old seems to actually enjoy using many of the previously disapproved behaviors in rapid sequence as a harassment. This situation is painful and does not need to happen.

Christiana, at eighteen months of age, was developing especially well, and, of course, she too wondered on a daily basis just how much power she had. One day, she and her mother were sitting on the kitchen floor facing each other. Her mother was peeling carrots, and Christiana was eating Cheerios from a plastic bowl. She ate a few, and then several more, and then she began taking them out of the bowl one at a time and slowly and deliberately dropping them onto the floor. Christiana made certain that her mother noticed what she was doing by staring at her steadily as she dropped each piece of cereal. Her mother told her not to drop the cereal on the floor and to pick up what she had dropped. Christiana ignored the instruction. In fact, she continued dropping the cereal, one piece at a time, all the while studying her mother's face. After saying a second time, in a calm and serious tone of voice, that the cereal had to be picked up, Christiana's mother watched while the child gently and deliberately tilted the whole bowl of perhaps thirty pieces onto the floor. The issue was joined. What we had here was a clear confrontation of wills.

Christiana moved out of the room while her mother continued to sit on the kitchen floor in front of the spilled Cheerios and the empty bowl. She came back five seconds later with a book and indicated that she would like to be read to, an activity ordinarily encouraged by her mother. Christiana's mother (following the strong recommendations of our staff) rejected the suggestion and said, "You have to pick up the Cheerios." Christiana looked at her and then wandered away. After a while, she checked into the kitchen again with a different book. Her mother was still sitting in front of the spilled Cheerios. Again her mother would not agree to a story session. It took close to ten minutes. Finally, the baby came back, sat down, took the bowl, and replaced all the Cheerios. Gentle reader, this was good parenting.

If Christiana had been in the habit of doing this sort of thing day in and day out, we would have been dealing with a situation that called for punishment. This was not that kind of situation. It was simply a straightforward instance of "experimentation with power." It is, however, not uncommon for a nineteen- or twenty-month-old child to engage in behaviors on a regular basis that simply shouldn't be tolerated. It is not at all abnormal for children at this age to smear food or to throw objects at their parents or to hit them, even in the face, which is, after all, a very inviting target as a parent bends over toward a child to make a point. A good deal of antisocial behavior can become established during this very special time of life. What to do?

## Prevention of Proximity—
## A Humane Way to Control
## a Fourteen- to Twenty-two-Month-Old Child

When I discussed the seven-and-one-half-to-fourteen-month period, I described a way to discourage bad habits that featured brief episodes of immobilization. We devised this method of punishment after determining that all ten- to fourteen-month-old babies hate being absolutely still, especially during diapering. Correspondingly, when it comes to the fourteen-to-twenty-two-month age range we advocate a control mechanism based on what is invariably unpleasant to children during this developmental period. We call it "prevention of proximity"—that is, not allowing your child to come near you.

From fourteen to twenty-four months of age, normal children need to spend much more time close to the special people in their lives than they did when they were six months younger or than they will when they're a year older. Eighteen-month-olds ordinarily have immediate access to one parent or another if that parent is nearby. Preventing such access quickly reveals how important it is to a child during this time of life.

When a behavior simply becomes intolerable during the fourteen- to twenty-four-month age range, here's what I recommend you do. You have to arrange for a situation where all doors to the room but one can be closed and where you have a gate handy that can be quickly installed in that open doorway. Most often, the kitchen is ideal for the purpose. If your child is doing something to test your authority that you feel goes too far, give her a second chance to stop, presuming that she didn't understand that she was being told to stop or didn't hear the message. (By the way, at this age chances are very high that she did hear the message and that she understood it as well.) Repeat the message one time, but only one time. If she persists, install the gate in the doorway to the room, pick her up, and put her on the other side of the gate, while saying in simple terms that she is being put behind the gate because she spilled the dog's food or was hitting the window or whatever. From the other side of the gate, she will be able to see you but not get to you.

Sooner or later, most fourteen- to twenty-four-month-old children react the same way. They begin to complain and shortly thereafter start to cry. Babies of this age hate being prevented from coming up close to their parents. You might think that they would simply turn around and find something to do elsewhere in the home. This does happen occasionally, particularly in the early stages of the fourteen-to-twenty-four-month phase, but it will not happen routinely as time goes on. What they will usually do is stand at the gate and show you they are unhappy.

Take a look at your watch. From the time the complaints start, give your daughter a good twenty- to thirty-second dose of the punishment. At the end of that time, approach her. After she has quieted a bit, make a short speech. "I'm going to let you back in the room with me, but if you bang your toy on the window again, I'm going to use the gate again." After five of six episodes the word "gate" acquires power, and just the threat of its use will often do the job.

There are situations where it isn't feasible to use a gate. The room may be part of an open floor plan, where the spaces connecting rooms are very wide. In one such instance, a clever mother whose sixteen-month-old refused to stop throwing food from the high chair simply turned her back to the child and announced that she would keep it turned until the baby stopped. It worked.

You may even find that confining the child to a playpen briefly will do the trick (until the child can climb out of it—

usually not before twenty months of age). The important point here is that prevention of immediate access to key people is usually very effective during the second half of the second year.

You will be able to shift to the use of rational methods of control toward the end of the second year, when most babies become able, for the first time, to consider alternatives. When a two-year-old continues to act unacceptably, you can explain in simple terms that if she continues to disobey, she will not be allowed to play with her favorite toy for the rest of the day. Chances are good, particularly if your preceding threats have been carried out, that the the newly thoughtful child will pause for a few moments, consider the consequences, and then accept your demand. That kind of appeal to reason will cut no ice at all, however, with an eighteen-month-old. Subrationality is still his style.

## Prevention of Proximity Versus "Time Out"

"Time out" has become a reasonably popular concept within parent education circles only within the last fifteen years or so. It appears to be an extension of practices that nursery school teachers have used for years with two-and-one-half- to five-year-old children. In the nursery school situation, when control is needed teachers may designate a chair, usually out of the center of things, where a child is sent for a period of time when she has been misbehaving.

People started advocating the use of "time out" for children in the infancy stage during the 1970s, as more programs for children under nursery school age were established and as advice to parents began to proliferate.

Some people have had some degree of success with the "time out" procedure with toddlers. In a sense, when you put a child outside of the kitchen and use a gate to keep him away from you, you are forcing him to take "time out." There is a big difference, however. "Time out," as in putting a child in a playpen or in his room and closing the door, rep-

resents not only prevention of proximity but also confinement. When you put a child behind a gate, where she can
see you but can't get to you, the message is considerably
more focused. The message to the child is centered on your
relationship. She isn't being confined. She is free to move
about the house. The only place she can't go is the most
important place in the home for a child at her stage of
development—close to you.

Also be advised that putting an eighteen- or nineteen-
month-old into a "time-out chair" simply won't work because
a child at this age won't stay there. The moment you turn
your back, he will get out of the chair and come after you.

A fourteen-month-old doesn't know much about how to
live in a family. Parents have to teach him how. The prime
time for accomplishing the major part of that task is the
fourteen-to-twenty-two-month period. If you are not firm, if
you yield when the child throws a tantrum, you are letting
him know that if he cries insistently enough he will overcome your resistance.

When Sonya not only insisted on coming into her parents' bed every night at 2:00 A.M., but began to demand
apple juice at 5:00 A.M., her parents devised a plan under
our guidance. The first night Sonya's father would go into
the nursery when the crying started or would take Sonya
back to her crib if she climbed out and came to their bed. He
would then set up a gate in the doorway to her room and sit
in a chair just outside. He would then make a short speech
to Sonya, telling her that it was sleeptime, that if she didn't
want to sleep that was okay, that she would have to stay in
her room no matter what, and that he would not play with
her. Sonya's mother did the same the next night. After the
better part of a week, Sonya got the message.*

*There are people who would find the behavior of Sonya's parents
abominable. Certainly, advocates of the "family bed" might even be
appalled. All parents should consider whether they are comfortable with
a firm limit-setting style or not. My research has convinced me that it is
the only effective way to guide a child successfully through the first two
years.

I hope I'm not misleading you as to how difficult this job is. Most of the parents we work with are intelligent and loving people who want the best for their children. Most of them do not like the notion of living with a spoiled child. At the same time, they don't like to see their baby unhappy. When push comes to shove, the urge not to see the baby unhappy can overcome the longer-term consideration that the child has to learn to accept that there are some things he cannot have immediately and that other people have rights that are sometimes more pressing than his own.

## MAINTAINING THE BALANCE AMONG THE PRIMARY INTERESTS

Given plenty of opportunities to satisfy her curiosity and to practice emerging motor skills between five and one-half and fourteen months of age, the baby enters into this special period of life with all three major interests—curiosity, motor activity, and socializing—in balance.

The vigorous expansion of the two primary nonsocial interests during the preceding months makes it easier to hold down development of an overly intense focus on the interpersonal struggle that so often develops, especially with first children, during the fourteen-to-twenty-four-month period of life.

### The Special Potential of Puzzles

Puzzles can be surprisingly useful during this period of your baby's life. The simplest kind of puzzle consists of a wooden board about three by eight inches wide, with three or four pieces, each with a small knob with which you can lift it out of its opening. Before sixteen months, you baby won't do much with even the simplest puzzle. He may explore it a bit. He will probably gum the pieces. He won't be able to learn to put the correct piece in place.

At about sixteen months, you can begin to teach your baby to do such puzzles correctly. Doing puzzles won't "help develop" her hand-eye skills. They don't need help. But when your baby manages to maneuver a puzzle piece into the right position, it drops into place in an obviously successful manner. There is no doubt about it. At that moment, your enthusiastic praise, combined with the clear evidence of success, effectively feeds your baby's sense of competence and pride.

It is important to introduce your baby to puzzles carefully to avoid frustration. Get his attention and then slowly demonstrate how to put a piece into its opening. Do this several times. Then place that piece as close as you can to where it should go, in other words, 99½ percent into the hole. Then give him a chance to move the piece the last fraction of an inch. If he succeeds right away or within a few tries, give him lots of praise. He will love it! Do it again, and again, and again. After a few times, you will find him enjoying the situation immensely.

Don't be surprised if, in spite of how close the piece is to falling in place, you baby clumsily moves it away. That's quite common in the beginning. If that happens, especially more than once or twice, he may begin to show that he is becoming frustrated. At the first sign of frustration, take the puzzle away and replace it with some other activity. Try again another day.

Most children can be introduced successfully to puzzles between sixteen and eighteen months. A tip for you: As your child's pleasure in mastering puzzles grows, you can keep in reserve one or two at his level of skill. After he has gone to sleep, you can put one he has never seen before in his crib. In the morning, he may find the puzzle and keep himself occupied with it for as much as a half hour. I'm sure you can use the extra sleep.

• • • •

## Part-Time Versus Full-Time Parenting

The fourteen-to-twenty-two-month period is a time when children, for reasons over which they have absolutely no control, work toward the completion of the attachment process. Intimately intertwined with the evolving attachment process is the regular, equally obligatory, experimentation with power. These two basic, all-powerful drives underlie the substantial increase in emotional intensity that develops during the second half of the second year of life between the baby and his principal adult, usually his mother. One unpleasant consequence can be the development of overly clingy behavior. Another can be the escalation of whining and tantrums. For all of these reasons (and more), we don't think that anybody should be home full-time with a baby during this phase. We strongly urge regular time away from the child during this stage.

Not only is this good for the mental health of the parent, but it also helps preserve a solid balance among the child's three primary interests—the social impulse, the interest in satisfying curiosity, and the enjoyment of motor activities. It should be clear now that paying attention to the balance of primary interests from five and one-half months on is quite important in successfully getting through the first two years. If the child hasn't been subjected to long periods of boredom between five and one-half months and seven and one-half months of age, an overly strong demand for social attention will not begin to develop. If the child from seven and one-half months to fourteen months has been given the opportunity to explore the home, rather than having been confined regularly to playpens, cribs, and small rooms, that freedom to explore, along with ready access to as many of the kitchen cabinets as possible, goes a long way toward feeding the child's curiosity and motor interests. These developing interests will hold down the overdevelopment of focus on the parents.

This is also a good time to take advantage of such simple programs as infant exercise groups. It is not that babies of this age need the exercise, but rather that these programs can broaden and enrich life in developmentally suitable ways. At the same time, they serve to relieve some of the pressure that builds up around parent-child interactions.

You can also take advantage of the emergence of interest in television and videos during this period. While some babies begin to show such interest much earlier, most stay with what is on the screen in a sustained fashion only from this stage on.

Some parents prefer to avoid television and video viewing altogether. My recommendation is to make use of it judiciously. There are some lovely videos that most children enjoy during the second year of life. Among others, I recommend *Meet Your Animal Friends, Baby Songs, Thomas the Tank Engine, 101 Dalmations,* and *Road Construction Ahead.* I believe limited exposure to such high-quality videos adds another dimension to the toddler's life and does not threaten his growing interest in books.

## SUMMARY

The fourteen-to-twenty-two-month period is generally the most stressful period in the early parenting process for typical, loving parents raising their first child. No matter how good a job you're doing, you're going to experience stress regularly. You will, after all, be dealing with a subrational creature whom you love very dearly. This creature is obliged, for reasons no one fully understands, to work out some sort of an agreement that stipulates the limits of her power and the rules by which she will live in your family.

I don't believe you can do a first-rate job of creating a desirable agreement without your baby occasionally becoming very unhappy with the limits you have set. I assure you that if you yield to that unhappiness on a regular basis you'll find that the price will be very high for all of you. If your child learns the core lesson that she is extremely precious and loved, and that her needs are very important, but that she is no more precious than anyone else in the world, nor are her needs more important than those of other people, especially yours, then you're likely to do just fine. Armed with the kind of information I've attempted to give you, which is based on work with large numbers of families of different kinds, you have an exciting opportunity to help your child develop into an absolutely wonderful two-year-old. Don't be surprised if the task is difficult. Don't be afraid to ask for help. And above all, don't try to do it all by yourself. Remember the goal: a reasonable twenty-two- to twenty-four-month-old child who spends most of every day living happily and with excitement and who simply radiates love, security, intelligence, imagination, and humor. What could be better?

## SIGNS THAT A NEW STAGE OF SOCIAL DEVELOPMENT IS BEGINNING

The beginnings of negativistic behavior can appear at any time from fourteen to eighteen months of age. The next stage of social development can begin as early as twenty-two months; more commonly it starts at twenty-four months, and sometimes much later. The reason is that the next stage begins when a child stops testing the authority of his parents and begins to be seriously interested in play with peers. If you have done a superb job of socializing your child during his first twenty-two months, what follows will be exciting and heavenly. Testing will disappear except when your child is ill or extremely tired, and you will be living with an agreeable, rational, wonderful companion. If you have merely done a terrific job, the new stage will not begin for another month or two. If things have not gone well, the normal tug of war with the negativistic nineteen-month-old may go on for several more months.

# Twenty-two to Thirty to Thirty-six Months—A Period of Incredible Enjoyment or Increasing Stress

## NORMAL SOCIAL DEVELOPMENT

THIS is payoff time. Parents will either be entering one of the most exciting and rewarding stages of parenthood or they will be in the soup. Although there are degrees, I have been impressed by how often parents get one result or the other, with rather few situations falling in between. Two-year-olds are usually either an absolute delight or not much fun at all to be with.

Whether a child has become spoiled or not becomes quite clear by the time she is two years old. Major differences in social styles among children become obvious and firmly entrenched by then. That's not to say that changes are impossible after the second birthday. No one has seriously studied this issue. In our own work, however, we have consistently found that delightful two-year-olds stayed delightful for at least several years thereafter, and unpleasant, self-centered two-year-olds showed similarly persistent patterns of behavior.

The pace of development during the period from twenty-two to thirty-six months is remarkably slow in comparison to that of the first twenty-two months. In order to survive, every baby has to begin to form an attachment to at least one older person immediately after birth. All babies are born with qualities that make it very likely that someone will fall in love with them (whether they become spoiled or not). All babies grow and change rapidly during the first two years. By the second birthday, the attachment process and the accompanying intense concentration on key people has either completely or mostly run its course.

By two years, babies have mastered basic body skills. They can walk, run, jump, and climb. They can use their hands skillfully. Two-year-olds have become capable of elementary reasoning. Their short-term memory is fully developed. Especially in the case of well-developed two-year-olds, the third year brings a gradual refinement of patterns that have become well established. The only major changes you are likely to see during the third year will take place in respect to your child's experiences with peers. Of course, you will also find exciting growth in the areas of language and intelligence, but the changes will be quantitative, not qualitative.

If, on the other hand, development during the first twenty-two months has not gone well, a baby's concentration on her key people not only does not diminish, it actually intensifies, and interest in peers remains minimal.

## THE DEVELOPMENT OF INTEREST IN PEOPLE

What the two-year-old is like in these respects depends very much on how successful socialization has been up to that point. In most homes the child, especially if he is a first child, will have received lots of love day in and day out. In many such homes, the child will have been regularly overindulged. In such situations, the child will have become overly self-centered and will not yet have fully resolved the attachment process. He will still be engaged in a day-to-day struggle for power with his parents. His "thoughts" on socialization might be expressed as follows: "I'm still working on this process with these folks. I've surely learned that I have a lot of influence over them. I've also learned that if I push really hard and go immediately to a scream or pathetic crying, I'm likely to get what I want. Interestingly, every once in a while they seem to get exasperated. They don't let me have what I want. Certainly when I'm outside and I start to head for the street, that really gets them. At that point, they stop me, and there's not a thing I can do, but in the house or when I'm out with them at a big store I get the sense that there are times when I really run the show. As for children my own age, they mean much less to me than my parents do. Once in a while, I'll run into one I can play with for a while as long as I get my own way, but otherwise I would just as soon pass."

In the case where there is a slightly older sibling, the following might be added: "I like her at times, but lots of other times she's nasty to me. I have found out, though, that a loud cry will often bring my mother over and that will stop my sister. At other times, if I can get ahold of her hair or get close enough to bite, I can get her back for some of the stuff I've had to put up with for a long time. All in all, I have mixed feelings about her."

In the case where there is an eighteen-month-old sibling, add the following: "Why did that creature have to show up in my house? Boy, does he make a difference, and I can't see that it is ever a difference for the better. I wish they would send him back. He used to be easy to push around. Now my mother seems to be on to me. She often stops me before I can get at him. To make matters worse, he's beginning to pick on me! And when he pulls my hair or bites me, it really hurts! I sure hope he's not going to be around much longer. I want it to be the way it used to be—just the three of us."

(Once again a reminder: Children don't think these things through, but this is what their behavior indicates.)

The other scenario is a much happier one. When things have gone very well, the two-year-old's behavior reveals an increasing interest and enjoyment in interacting with children his own age, provided that they too are well developed. That's a very important proviso. If child type B (nicely developed) runs into child type A (spoiled), he generally gets out of the way in a hurry. If child type B runs into another child type B, some precocious and extremely enjoyable friendships can begin to develop. In other words, "I'm interested in those folks out there my own age, but I'm gradually learning that they come in all sizes and shapes and that I've got to be selective. As for my parents, they're just great. We really enjoy each other. We don't argue very much, and I look forward to spending time with them every day."

## The Direction of Social Interest

One clear sign, then, of how well the socialization process has gone is seen in the child's direction of interest in people. When progress is good, the two-year-old will enjoy interacting with all people, with the exception of closely spaced siblings (older or younger). Even the beautifully developed two-year-old can't handle the emotions involved in living with either a twelve-month-old competitor or a three- or four-year-old who's been his long-term nemesis. This is too much to expect.

In the case of the chronically overindulged two-year-old, the direction of social interest remains narrowly focused on his mother or father, depending on how the child-rearing assignment has been handled.

Corinne was a remarkably bright two-year-old. Her language far exceeded that of the average four-year-old. Unfortunately, her associated high level of intelligence, along with her fixation on her mother, frequently made life miserable for both parents. During home visits, our staff noted that Corinne showed almost none of the typical interest of children her age in the visitor or her father. Her unwavering purpose throughout the hour was to monopolize her mother's attention. To do so she had developed several tactics. She would climb onto her mother's lap, facing her, and regularly force her mother's head in her direction to achieve and maintain eye contact. She would demand her mother's participation in her activities, even though her mother was trying to hold a conversation with the visitor. She had developed two transparently phony physical attention-getting practices—mild hysteria and gagging. The roots of these behaviors had been clearly visible from the time Corinne was nine or ten months old.

Corinne was hopeless with peers on the playground as well as at home. Her mother reported that Corinne hovered near her and found unfamiliar children threatening. When attempts were made by other mothers in her group to get the children to play together, Corinne was embarrassingly strident and uncooperative. In each instance, the effort was called off. At twenty-seven months of age (when our program ended), the only important person in Corinne's life was still her mother.

## THE DEVELOPMENT OF SPECIAL SOCIAL ABILITIES

As early as twenty-two months of age, the child who is developing well starts to interact smoothly with peers, provided that the other child is also socially mature. As talented as the well-developed twenty-two-month-old may be, you should not expect her to be able to cope with most others of that age. The reason is that most other twenty-two-month-olds will not yet be ready for peer play.

On the whole, twenty-two months is very early for children to interact with each other in a civil manner. You can confirm that statement for yourself by visiting a few nursery schools that admit children between two and three years old; genteel behavior among such children isn't expected much before thirty months. If you follow the guidelines I have been describing, your child is very likely to be one of the delightful minority who socialize easily with agemates as early as twenty-two months.

You should be mindful of the following realities. If you have had success and your child has become a delightful, unspoiled twenty-two-month old, he will be unusual in that respect, and you will have to be selective when looking for social experiences for him. If you try a play group, don't be surprised if another child his age begins to grab his toys or hit or shove him. Such behaviors are perfectly normal for the typical twenty-two-month-old. Of course, it is even more likely with a younger toddler. Do not try to teach him how to cope with such nasty behavior. Remove him from the situation and find another that works. In one case, we had a family arrange for their socially mature twenty-two-month-old to be placed in a group of older twos. He got along just fine. In fact, he was soon able to enjoy attending that nursery school five days a week from 9:00 A.M. to 3:00 P.M. Very few children of that age look forward to going to "school" every weekday. He did. As with most twenty-two-month-olds, a socially advanced child will almost always enjoy being with three- or four-year-olds.

Interacting effectively with peers means being able to express both positive and negative feelings to another child, being able to take turns leading and following another child, and being able to compete without harsh feelings.

It is quite common for a nicely developed three- or four-year-old to approach another child and say, "You're nice. I like you." On the other hand, the same child may tell another, "Please leave me alone. I'm busy now, and you're bothering me." Such children act as though they know they are likable. They don't exert any special effort in order to be liked.

The ability to express feelings toward another child is no different from what we talked about in connection with the emergence of that kind of social behavior toward parents during the last few months of the first year of life.

Leading and following another child can be seen as taking turns in play.

The roots of leadership lie in the first use of the cry to intentionally affect a parent's behavior when a baby is about six months of age. The initiating of games at eleven months and "directing" behaviors during the fourteen- to twenty-four-month period evolve directly into acting as a leader with agemates.

Jennifer revealed an energetic and enthusiastic style early in her second year. As fate would have it, her parents were friendly with another couple in our program who had a rather quiet, exceptionally agreeable little boy of the same age. As the second year transpired, Jennifer's social development was unusually rapid. By the time she was eighteen months old, she would routinely orchestrate her play with Ryan. She would decide who would play with which toys, where they would play, and when they would switch activities. It was clear that her leadership potential was unlimited!

By two years, she was into the habit of guiding her father through his morning routine. "Get up now, Daddy." "Put on your robe." "Take a shower now, Daddy."

On my last home visit with Jennifer, she spent most of the hour "feeding" her parents, two of her dolls, and me. At times she used an electronic thermometer to "take everyone's temperature."

This delightful pattern of activity is quite common with well-developed children as they enter their third year. It illustrates not only leadership ability but also the increasing complexity of make-believe or pretend play, which had its origins in brief "telephone conversations" shortly after the first birthday.

Good socialization includes the ability to follow another child as well as lead. Parents who do a good job setting limits during the period from seven and one-half months to twenty-four months make it easy for the child to let a playmate have a turn at leading their joint activities.

A child who is not developing well will not display these abilities until much later, if at all. If you are still hung up in your struggle for power with your parents, enjoyable play with peers simply doesn't get a chance to happen very much during the third year. Play with other twenty-four-, twenty-six-, or twenty-eight-month-old children generally represents a junior version of the power struggle at home (but without parental love or restraint). Rarely does such a child tell another that she's nice or that she really likes him. Sadly for the spoiled child, play with peers soon degenerates into grabbing, hitting, and crying.

In our early research, we noted consistently that well-developed three- to six-year-olds, noting another child's creation, such as a drawing or clay figure, might say with enthusiasm, "I can make a better one!" and then get to work. When they finished, however, they never took their product to the first child and said, "See, I told you I could make a better one than you!" The statement "I can make a better one" was simply the combination of a judgment about the quality of the creation and an expression of self-confidence. The child knew what a better one would be, and she was quite sure that she could produce it. She was in no way trying to show up or put down the other child.

Matthew was seated at a table, painting. Though we had been filming him, he knew we were "busy" and that he was, in effect, alone. After a few quiet minutes, during which he worked more or less steadily, he paused, held his brush up, and said, to no one in particular, "I'm doing a good job!" This kind of confidence that he is capable of first-rate work is a characteristic you can look for during your child's third year.

## THE DEVELOPMENT OF A SOCIAL STYLE

Research on the staying power of the personality of a two-year-old child is slim. I have been impressed, however, with how stable the patterns of social behavior have become by the second birthday, particularly when things have gone well. We rarely have seen wonderful two-year-olds turn nasty later, at least over their next few years. We have seen mildly overindulged two-year-olds improve considerably during the third year of life. On the other hand, children who are grossly overindulged during their first two years not only are no fun for anyone, but they appear to be remarkably resistant to change for at least the next year or two. How many of these early patterns will persist into later childhood and beyond is anyone's guess, but I would rather see the process go well in the early formative stages than take my chances.

### Testing—An Important Indicator

You will know when the struggle for authority is over when your baby stops testing you. It is as simple as that. Testing is to be expected frequently between fourteen and twenty-two months of age, regardless of how well the child is developing. Testing will begin to recede at around eighteen or twenty months of age under the best circumstances. Under the very best of circumstances, it is over by twenty-two months of age. In such happy instances, the twenty-two-month-old child seems to be saying, "Okay, now I understand just what I can do and what I can't do when I am with my parents. Now I understand what the boundaries are. Now I know that I am a highly valued person whose needs are going to be met most of the time, but there will be other times when there will be a delay or I can't have what I want. That's a pretty good deal. I think I'll live with it."

If a child is still testing the authority of a parent at two years of age, everyone is in for trouble. I remember vividly a recent airplane trip where a child just under three demonstrated very powerfully that he was gifted in annoying his mother. He knew a variety of ways to get to her, and he used a fair number of them repeatedly during this trip. He insisted on standing in his seat and throwing his books down the aisle. Despite his mother's many requests, commands, and entreaties, he simply refused to sit down and behave himself. Each time he threw a book, his mother would retrieve it and give it back to him, while suggesting that he sit down and read it. It was clear that he much preferred annoying her and holding her full attention to sitting down and being agreeable. He seemed to actually enjoy tormenting her. Yet I have no doubt that at five months of age he was a gorgeous, endearing baby. I felt great sympathy for that woman.

It would be very nice if by twenty-four months of age all children finished testing and exploring their power and then turned into delightful, rational beings. Unfortunately, that remarkable situation happens in only a minority of cases. Far more common is the scenario in which the child continues to test his parents right on through the second birthday and well into the third year of life. If poor outcomes were rare, of course, there would be no need for this book. Indeed, our early research finding that unpleasant two-year-olds were extremely common has been thoroughly reconfirmed in the intervening years.

Then, too, if there is a younger sibling in the home, the entire situation becomes even worse, particularly if that younger child has reached the crawling stage. Lately, this difficult situation occurs much more often as families put off having children until they are well into their thirties. The biological clock ticks, and many families feel they must have their children close together if they want more than one.

When the older child has become significantly spoiled, sibling rivalry problems are magnified dramatically. If you want to see a two-and-a-half-year-old who has really turned sour, just identify a spoiled, overindulged one-and-a-half-year-old who has a newborn sibling; then watch the next year transpire. What you'll find is an increasingly unhappy older child who by two and one-half not only has been struggling with his parents about his own power but also has had to move over and take second place to a younger sibling. This creates an extremely difficult situation for all involved—the parents, the new child, and, of course, the person with the greatest difficulty, the older child. If close spacing cannot be avoided, you can reduce the difficulties somewhat by not overindulging the older child. But there is no way to completely solve the dilemma.

The principal purpose of this book is to help prevent such outcomes in as many future situations as possible. As has been the case in my previous writings, the people who find my work most useful are those who learn about our findings early in the child-rearing process. If it is any consolation to the others, they should know that the mother of my children and I had none of this information when we raised our four children. At one time we had three children under three years of age. In retrospect, that was clearly unwise.

It is one thing to deal with a fifteen- or sixteen-month-old who is resistant and tests your authority. A twenty-four-month-old is, however, a much more formidable antagonist. In addition, as the weeks go by after the second birthday, the need becomes increasingly pressing to bring the child around to an acceptable style of behavior toward family members. At the same time, the difficulty of doing so grows. I believe that the effects of the previous pattern of overindulgence in the two-year-old can and must be removed by the age of two and one-half years.

Several important factors make this necessary. First, as the weeks go by, the undesirable behaviors become increasingly habitual and therefore resistant to change. I should also point out that by this stage, parents often have reached the end of their rope. They have struggled with a chronically demanding child since he was seven months old. Their own patterns of response and control have firmed up, even though they don't work well. Some parents have resorted to spanking. All in all, their task is tougher and their ability to cope has diminished.

Second, and just as important, is the fact that during the third year of life children usually begin to form their first friendships with peers. To the extent that a thirty-month-old child has been spoiled, other children will not be inclined to play with or like him. Spoiled thirty-month-olds usually refuse to share toys or snacks or, for that matter, anything! They tend to scream a lot and are quick to hit or shove another child when their desires are not complied with immediately. They are also not inclined to take turns. All in all, they don't make attractive companions.

Finally, children who have been overindulged are not happy children. They are, in fact, likely to be chronically dissatisfied.

When the child-rearing process goes well, and I assure you it can, we find parents who are about as happy with their children as parents ever get to be, at least during the first years of life. A child who has stopped struggling with his parents at twenty-two to twenty-four months of age is also a child with a well-functioning mind. This development enables him to become a much more interesting person than he was a year earlier. He is now able to generate original observations. He is now able to show humor. This potent, newfound capacity to use the mind to manipulate ideas and to think, along with the usual explosion of expressive language during the last months of the second year, makes for dramatic and exciting changes. Instead of verbal interchanges consisting of commands, resistance, and threats, you can enjoy extraordinarily pleasurable conversations with your child. Perhaps what so impresses one is the awareness that so much is going on inside the head of a child who is so small and has been around for such a limited time. It is truly a mind-boggling experience.

## WHEN THINGS HAVE NOT GONE WELL—A CHRONIC TUG OF WAR

What about the twenty-four-month-old who is still engaged in the power struggle with her parents? Remember, the origins of her social style lie back in the sixth or seventh month of life. Expecting to correct in a few weeks the behavior of a chronically complaining, unhappy, overindulged two-year-old is unrealistic. For parents who find themselves in such unhappy circumstances, I can only offer my previous principles of effective child-rearing and an admonition. The sooner you teach your child to respect your rights, the better. The longer the unsatisfactory situation prevails, the more difficult it becomes to correct.

Parents of a spoiled two-year-old will have their work cut out for them for at least six more months. Starting at two and one-half or at least three years of age, with any luck at all they will be able to begin the process of orienting a child toward children her own age. Once the child begins to focus less on her parents and more on the outside world, the pressure diminishes. It does not disappear. A two- to two-and-one-half-year-old who hasn't developed well socially is no fun on an airplane, causes grief in restaurants and supermarkets, and in general is very tough to take. That third year is when a substantial percentage of all children are inclined to throw tantrums and in other ways be difficult to deal with. This is precisely why we have the term "terrible twos."

•  •  •

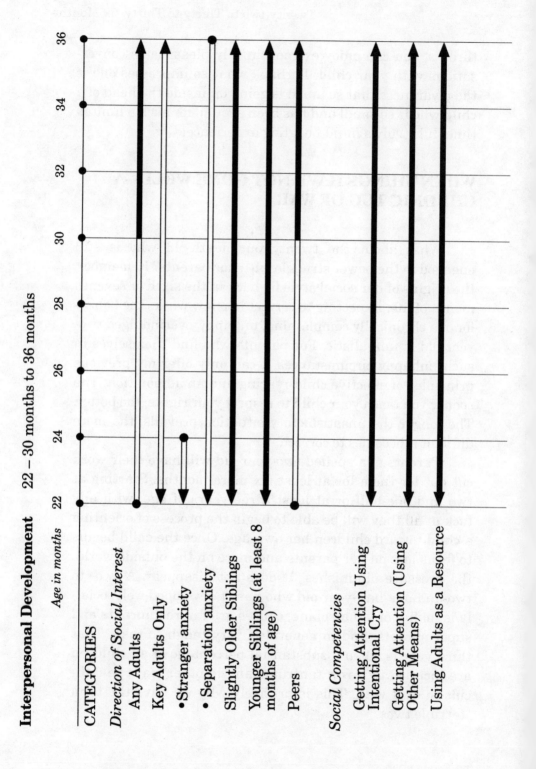

**Interpersonal Development** 22 – 30 months to 36 months

*Age in months*

36  34  32  30  28  26  24  22

**CATEGORIES**

*Direction of Social Interest*

Any Adults

Key Adults Only

• Stranger anxiety

• Separation anxiety

Slightly Older Siblings

Younger Siblings (at least 8 months of age)

Peers

*Social Competencies*

Getting Attention Using Intentional Cry

Getting Attention (Using Other Means)

Using Adults as a Resource

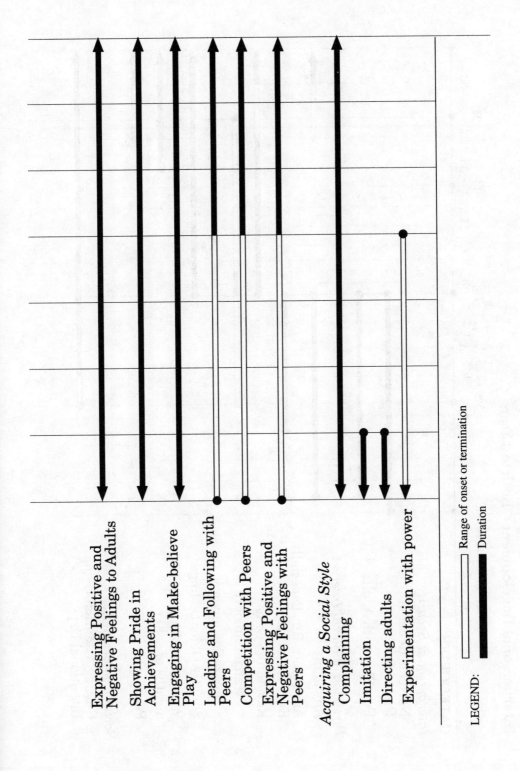

Expressing Positive and
Negative Feelings to Adults

Showing Pride in
Achievements

Engaging in Make-believe
Play

Leading and Following with
Peers

Competition with Peers

Expressing Positive and
Negative Feelings with
Peers

*Acquiring a Social Style*

Complaining

Imitation

Directing adults

Experimentation with power

LEGEND: ☐ Range of onset or termination

■ Duration

# Interpersonal Development   Birth to 3 Years

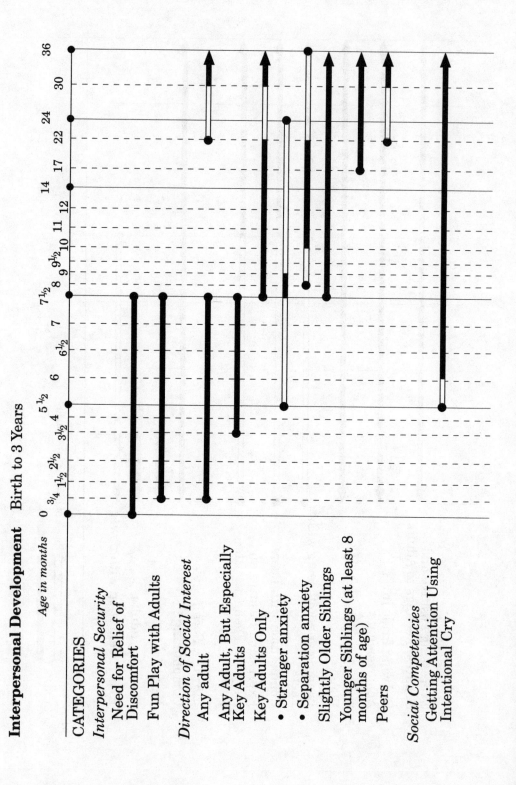

Getting Attention (Other Means)

Using Adults as a Resource

Expresing Positive and Negative Feelings to Adults

Showing Pride in Achievements

Engaging in Make-believe Play

Leading and Following with Peers

Expressing Positive and Negative Feelings with Peers

*Acquiring a Social Style*

Complaining

Taking Small Mishaps in Stride

Acquisition of Good and Bad Habits

Learning to Insist on Having One's Own Way

Imitation

Initiating Games

Directing Adults

Experimentation with Power

LEGEND: ☐ Range of onset or termination    ■ Duration

## WHEN THE PROCESS HAS GONE WELL AFTER TWENTY-TWO TO TWENTY-FOUR MONTHS

If you have done a superb job of parenting during your child's first twenty-two months (and had good luck), your child will have stopped testing and entered into a very special and wonderful stage of life. If you have merely done a very fine job, your child may continue the struggle for authority until he is twenty-four months old. In either case, your twenty-two- to twenty-four-month-old will be one of nature's miracles. The whole family will revel in such a happy, talented creature. The child will be ready to explore the world of peers. She will have a fine time playing with three-, four-, and five-year-olds as well.

If you have trouble finding agreeable playmates for your child, don't feel as if your twenty-two- to twenty-four-month-old is missing something vital. In my judgment, if you continue to provide interesting activities for her to engage in during the next months, she will be deprived of nothing of developmental significance. Indeed, if she never goes to a nursery school but continues to have a rich, loving environment, she will do just fine. As the second year transpires, she will, however, become increasingly interested in children her own age. Fortunately, month by month more and more children will become mature enough for enjoyable play.

### What to Do About Nursery School

A good nursery school experience makes sense for a child beginning as early as twenty-two months. The reason is that interest in agemates emerges as a major factor sometime between then and the third birthday. Readiness for nursery experience or related activities such as play groups and group care varies considerably according to how the socialization process has gone. Although a child can be ready at twenty-two months, the majority are not until at least thirty months. You will find a substantial diversity of opinions on this subject.

Even though it is by no means essential for good development, I am a strong advocate of nursery school experience. I have two reasons for encouraging it. First and foremost, most children enjoy going to a well-run school. It makes sense when they are ready. Second and especially important, if there is a younger sibling at home, it makes life easier for parents and for both children.

Whether it be nursery school, a play group, or group care, certain guidelines should be followed. Safety is primary, but not only in respect to the physical facility. The younger the children, the more real is the danger of one child hurting another. Do not underestimate this possibility. Both hazards will be minimal if the people in charge are capable and experienced. Beware of those who claim that their nursery school will provide important educational benefits for your children. Research has demonstrated repeatedly that no preschool program yet devised can convey lasting benefits either in academic areas such as language or intelligence or, for that matter, in regard to social abilities. If a professional promises such benefits, her judgment is suspect.

In my opinion, a small play group can be just as rewarding for your child as a nursery school. For one thing, children under three years of age do not engage in group activities. They play with one child at a time. Limiting any such experience during the third year of life to five half days seems more reasonable to me than eight- or nine-hour full-week regimens. If your child seems eager to go to play group or nursery school most mornings, you are probably doing the right thing.

# CHAPTER 6

# Special Topics

## PRINCIPAL HAZARDS TO WATCH OUT FOR

THE longer we work with families and study the relation-ships among various child-rearing styles and social styles of children, the more clear it becomes that certain obstacles to the best results are common. What follows are our best judgments on what they are and how to cope with them.

### Special Concerns About the Baby's Health

Understandably, first-time parents worry, especially during their baby's early months, about her health. Is she normal? God forbid that there is anything wrong. She's so small and weak. As time goes by and parents become more confident, these kinds of fears decline. This anxiety exists even when absolutely nothing is wrong with the baby. It is both normal and totally understandable. Who wouldn't be alarmed when his new baby, resting quietly (for a change), suddenly thrusts his arms and legs outward and starts to cry? Unless you have been forewarned about the spontaneous startles of the first three months, no reasonable person would ignore such frightening behavior.

In some situations, though, when there are indications that there is or might be something wrong, the anxiety level is higher and affects the child-rearing practices of the parents. Particularly noteworthy in this respect are premature birth, late parenting, chronic illness on the part of the baby, and prolonged colic.

## Prematurity

It has long been known that prematurity often results in developmental delays. Parents of premature infants need to be concerned about the possibility that during the child's early life the effects of prematurity may not completely disappear. In recent years, the medical profession has made remarkable strides in coping with early births. We are seeing a reduction of deficits in development and an increase in the survival rate of smaller and smaller babies. The reduction of deficits is very good news. Nevertheless, a baby born at two, three, or even four pounds remains more at risk than a full-term baby and will certainly develop more slowly than the average baby.

It is natural to be overprotective of your premature child, especially during the first two years. Like many parents of premature babies, you may view your baby as more fragile than most and therefore in need of special treatment.

Unfortunately, this understandable perception can make it harder to avoid spoiling your child. The difficulty is often most clearly revealed in connection with feeding. If your baby is underweight because of prematurity, you hope that she'll catch up to normal standards quickly. This desire is very reasonable, yet at mealtimes it may render you less able to deal with a misbehaving ten-month-old than would otherwise be the case.

Many seven- to eight-month-old babies drop food from their high chairs, especially once their appetite has been somewhat sated. As Piaget explained, such behavior is a normal part of the evolution of interest in practicing hand-eye skills and studying the movements of objects through space. As such, dropping food from the high chair turns out to be a normal step in the development of intelligence.

Toward the end of the first year, dropping pieces of food off the side of the high chair is motivated not by an innocent interest in the paths of motion of objects but rather by curiosity about your objections to such behavior. Now you are dealing with something that often develops into a bad habit.

What to do? My advice for all full-term babies has been for parents to take a firm stand and end the meal if the baby has been told twice to stop throwing the food on the floor and hasn't stopped. My advice for parents of a modestly premature baby is the same.

However, if you are the parents of a premature baby, that advice will probably be very difficult to follow. If you are extremely concerned about the of food your baby is eating, ending a meal to make it clear to your baby that you will not tolerate her food throwing can be very difficult.

We always advise parents to make certain that their medical practitioner agrees with us. We believe that even a child born with modest prematurity will not be harmed when an occasional meal is ended abruptly in order for the parents to discourage this common kind of bad habit. In every case to date, we have found no disagreement. After four or five very short meals, from which they go away hungry, most ten-month-old babies stop throwing food onto the floor.

Fortunately, most premature babies have caught up with full-term infants by nine or ten months of age.

## Late Parenting

Today many people are having their first children when they are well past their mid-thirties. Because of the wide publicity about the increased likelihood of health problems and genetic defects of children born to "older" women, such parents tend to be as vulnerable as those who have premature infants. Often the first baby is the only baby such parents believe they will have. As a result, older first-time parents are sometimes more overprotective than would otherwise be the case.

Older first-time parents often overreact to the minor bumps and bruises of the seven- or eight-month-old child, thereby reinforcing the tendency of the baby to cry considerably more than she otherwise would. It becomes more difficult in such circumstances to teach the baby to take minor discomforts in stride. In general, parents who have their children later in life tend to treat them as somewhat more fragile than necessary. They are also inclined to be more lenient than other parents when it comes to issues of control.

## Chronic Illness

Children who suffer from more than the average number of physical ailments during infancy also cause special concern to their parents. Unfortunately, even in the best of circumstances some children are especially vulnerable to any number of diseases, some of which are life-threatening, during their first year. When an infant spends time in a hospital repeatedly or in other ways requires regular medical attention for conditions that could be serious, most parents become even more vulnerable to fears about the baby's well-being. This vulnerability doesn't make things any easier for parents when they have to be firm about their baby's misbehavior.

## Prolonged Colic

Most babies suffer regularly from mysterious digestive problems during their first two to two and one-half months of life, and some suffer more than others. Sometimes this condition extends well beyond the first ten weeks, but it rarely lasts beyond six months of age.

A baby of any age who is suffering through an episode of digestive discomfort will show that she feels miserable. Naturally, these babies are picked up, rocked, and soothed much more than the average. Because the colicky baby experiences far more of such comforting episodes than the norm, it does seem to me that colicky babies become more demanding for attention during their third to eighth months than other babies. In my judgment, parents have no choice but to continue to try to make a colicky baby more comfortable, even though in the process the baby will become more demanding. When the colic subsides, there will be plenty of time to correct the problem of excessive complaints. Whether or not you have a colicky baby is one of many factors that is strictly a matter of chance.

## OTHER COMMON OBSTACLES

### Guilt

For a wide variety of reasons, many of today's babies are not spending the majority of each day in close proximity to their mothers. Until twenty years ago, this was not the traditional lifestyle; most mothers stayed home full-time with their babies. Today, no matter how modern a young couple may be, they cannot completely avoid a sense of guilt if during the first year or two of their baby's life they deviate much from the earlier pattern. The person who bears the weight of the guilt most heavily is the child's mother, and that guilt is almost invariably counterproductive.

Guilt that one isn't doing enough for one's baby, that one isn't spending enough time with him, that as a result he may love one less—these feelings tend to show up when the time comes to set limits and be firm with the baby. Few first-time parents are unmoved when their baby cries because he is unhappy. It is particularly heartbreaking when both parents are away from the baby for eight and one-half to nine hours a day, five days a week, and want so badly to have an especially good time with that baby when they are together. In those situations, the desire to make up for short hours together predisposes the parents to be overindulgent or to tolerate behavior that would otherwise be judged unacceptable. The task, then, of avoiding a spoiled three-year-old is made more difficult.

## Adoption

Parents who adopt a baby have an especially strong need to have that baby realize how much she is loved and to have that baby love them back. These factors make avoiding overindulgence more difficult. Adoptive parents need to be aware of their extra vulnerability in this regard.

The age of the baby when you receive her can have substantial significance. If she hasn't been with you from her first days, you are not likely to ever know much about the details of her early experiences. Usually, late adoption does not mean that the child has been overindulged. Although I am sure there are many exceptions, overindulgence is far more likely to come from typical kinds of early parenting experiences rather than from the kinds of circumstances that may occur in problematic foster care or in cases of parental neglect.

You may be especially inclined to overindulge your baby if you have not adopted her within her first months of life. At the very least, without having any detailed information about what has happened to her before she came to you, you will probably tend to bend over backwards in dealing with her.

The older the baby is at adoption, the more you should prepare yourselves for the possibility of pre-existing problems over which you may have little influence. It is best to adopt as early as possible. If you have not, then lavish love and attention on your child, but at the same time always try to make it clear that as loved and valued as she is, she must respect your needs, too. You can exercise "healthy selfishness" while simultaneously giving your child a solid sense that she is very precious to you.

## Parent's Temperament

When a baby between eight and twenty-four months of age faces opposition from one of his parents, sooner or later the baby is going to cry. Babies in such situations can cry out of anger or they can cry out of unhappiness. Crying out of anger bothers parents, but when the baby cries because he's unhappy, it breaks their hearts.

In our work, we have found that parents vary substantially as to how they are affected by their baby's tears. Some find that it is an unhappy situation but that since it is their job to make it clear the baby can't have or do some things, they manage to resist yielding to the crying when they feel they need to. Others are equally aware of what they ought to do, but emotionally they just can't deal with the situation. The result is that they tend to yield to the baby's unhappiness considerably more readily than do other parents. The long-term result of that style of parenting is an overindulged child.

We have found a possible test of the degree of "softness" of parents in a film that we use in our parent-education program. It is called *Care of the Infant: Human and Animal*. It features the work of an animal trainer named Ivan Tors.

In trying to demonstrate the remarkable differences among mammalian species that surround the birth of a new baby, the film begins with a typical hospital delivery of a human, followed by the birth of an antelope on the plains of Africa. The hospital scene shows a half dozen adults around a delivery table handling the various functions that go on during an ordinary delivery in a first-rate hospital. A lot of people are providing a lot of assistance. During the delivery process, a great deal of attention is paid to the movement of the infant through the cervical canal. Doctors hover over the mother's midsection expectantly, ready to use forceps, perform an episiotomy, or even do a cesarean section if it becomes necessary. The obstetrical team is there, ready and willing to do whatever is needed.

Once the baby's head has made it out into the open, his shoulders are gently eased out. The umbilical cord is then clamped. The baby's respiratory passages are drained to assist him in starting to breathe. The baby is taken to a nearby table and cleaned. He is then brought to his mother's arms. After the parents enjoy the miracle of their baby's arrival, the mother may put the baby to her breast. Soon there will be a careful examination of the baby to make sure all is well. If something abnormal is found, treatment will be provided immediately.

A few days later, mother and baby go home, where for many years his parents and perhaps grandparents will do everything they can to help that baby become a happy and successful member of society.

The camera then switches to the African veldt. The baby gnu (the antelope) is seen dropping from its mother's vaginal opening to the ground. There are thousands of adult gnus in the general area, but not one pays any attention to the baby. The baby lies in a heap on the ground, moving his four limbs here and there in an inept attempt to get up. He clearly doesn't do very well at the job, and it takes him quite a while to get even halfway up. Once he does so, he immediately falls back to the ground. The camera then scans over to the surrounding bush, where a number of lions (obviously hungry) are apparently watching and waiting. They have sniffed the distinctive aroma of the amniotic fluid!

A breathless narrator, speaking in hushed tones, explains that the baby gnu must not only stand up in the next few minutes but must then run off with the rest of the herd if it is to survive. The baby gnu rises frantically and clumsily to a standing position at least a half dozen times, and every time it does it falls to the ground in a few moments. The situation looks hopeless.

In virtually any audience of parents, a certain amount of tension develops at about this time. Nobody wants to see that baby gnu left behind by the herd to be, of course, dealt with by the lions.

As parent groups watch this film, they clearly find it quite compelling. What is also clear is that the amount of tension they feel varies considerably among the participants. Some parents find parts of the film almost too much to bear. Remember Sonya, the eighteen-month-old who insisted on sleeping with her parents and then began to demand apple juice at 5:00 A.M.? Her mother and father found the film nerve-racking, as did the parents of both Henry (the houseplant squeezer) and Corinne (the little girl who held her mother's head to ensure eye contact). In our work, this kind of response to the film's suspenseful moments is quite common. The people who become most tense have invariably been among the kindest and gentlest we have worked with. Such parents seem to have more trouble than others in avoiding overindulging their children. By the way, the baby gnu survives!

What I'm trying to get across is that a certain capacity for firmness makes it a lot easier to do a first-rate job in avoiding creating an overindulged three-year-old than if you are temperamentally a very soft person. Having been in the field of psychology for more than thirty-six years, I believe these qualities lie at the core of a person's temperament and are not easily modified. I have a particular affection for gentle people, but I do believe the child-rearing task is more difficult for them than for the rest of us who are somewhat more hard-hearted.

What can you do if you happen to be an extremely sensitive person who crumbles at even the thought of your baby being unhappy? All you can do is (a) be mindful of my conclusion that your temperament is an important element in the child-rearing situation, and (b) with your partner's assistance, do everything you possibly can to control its limiting effects.

So, for example, almost invariably from nine or ten months on, parents will encounter circumstances when they aren't sure whether they're being too firm or not firm enough with their babies. What we tell parents whom we judge to be unusually gentle is: "When in doubt, you can safely assume you are inclined to be overindulgent, and you should therefore try to draw the line a bit more firmly." Of course, in a parent education program such as New Parents as Teachers, with a trained home visitor coming into the home and observing the parent-child relationship on a monthly basis, it is relatively easy for a parent to get input. Parents on their own don't have that luxury.

Being able to view other parents in action can help. Indeed, in all of our work we strongly emphasize the desirability of gaining perspective on your own situation as parents by observing whenever possible as many families like yours as you can. An objective and experienced perspective is one of the major differences between professionals and parents. For a family not in a first-rate program (and that's nearly all families, unfortunately), parent support groups can be very helpful. It is especially important that you deal with this issue during the baby's six- to twenty-four-month period of life. In the meantime, please consider that the degree to which the socializing job goes well will depend in part on the primary caretaker's temperament. Usually, it is the mother's temperament that is most influential, because she is generally the person who takes on the major part of the child-rearing task (even if she works out of the home). However, the father's temperament can become the major factor if he becomes the principal caregiver from the early months on. The amount of influence of an adult's temperament on the baby's development depends on how soon and how often he or she becomes a major factor in a baby's daily life.

## Common Conditions That Make It Difficult to Satisfy a Baby's Curiosity and Motor Interests

It is important for all babies from seven or eight months to three years of age to be able to pursue their three major interests—satisfying curiosity, mastering the body and related challenges such as hand-eye skills, and socializing. One very clear sign of a spoiled two-year-old is when the social interest dominates curiosity and enjoyment of motor activities. A central part of your job throughout the period between seven and one-half and twenty-four months of age is to keep these different interests growing and in balance.

Often family circumstances make the job of balancing interests more difficult. Limited space to explore is one such circumstance. Every newly crawling baby wants fervently to explore, but how much exploring she can do is up to you. You will decide whether she has to stay in the kitchen or living room with you, or is allowed on the stairs or may roam from room to room. You will decide whether she will have access to the contents of the kitchen cabinets. If you live in a small apartment or house, it will be somewhat more difficult to provide many opportunities for exploration than it would be if you had more space. Interestingly, no matter how small the housing space, babies find lots of situations that interest them. As long as parents use some ingenuity and care in making as much of the space available to them as possible, they will be intrigued. If a baby doesn't have opportunities to roam from room to room and explore diverse objects and spaces, her attention may very well become overly oriented toward the person who is nearby. You can hardly blame her.

You should take full advantage of the special value of

your kitchen. During her six- to twenty-four-month period of life, your baby will spend more time in the kitchen than in any other part of your home. Once babies become able to move around on their own, kitchens become more important in the child-rearing process, especially in avoiding spoiling, than one might suspect. A half dozen kitchen cabinets, a few drawers, and a pantry area or a storage closet (all made safe, of course) can keep a baby solidly engaged for long periods of time, day after day. This is particularly true during the eight- to eighteen-month period, an especially important time for the socializing process. And access to the wonderland of the kitchen, unlike the toy world, is free!

Another universally appealing and cost-free part of some homes is the stairs. It is a very unusual baby who doesn't begin to show a very strong interest in climbing stairs sometime between eight and eleven months of age, and most often between nine and ten months. Install a gate on the lip of the third step, thereby ensuring no falls from more than eighteen inches; then place some sort of cushion or thick padding on the floor at the foot of the stairs. Your baby will delight in the opportunity to practice climbing those stairs, and you need not fear that he will hurt himself.

Not long ago, I was conducting a home visit with a family where the first floor of the apartment consisted of a 12-foot-square living room and a small kitchen. Daniel, an adorable ten-month-old, began to crawl from the living room toward the kitchen. His mother saw where he was headed and quickly moved to put a chair across the kitchen doorway so that he could not enter. Later I asked Daniel's mother why she did what she did. Her answer was, "I wouldn't be able to see him when he went into the kitchen." Two factors were at work here. The first was that Daniel's mother was somewhat on the overprotective end of the scale. The second was that Daniel's parents had not as yet done much to safety-proof the kitchen. They were missing an excellent, free opportunity to give Daniel chances to satisfy his curiosity. In the process, they were channeling most of his energy toward his mother and forcing her to cope with Daniel's every-increasing demands for her attention.

Most kitchens are easily made into a wonderland for children between the ages of eight or nine months and two years. They can be very dangerous for such children, too, so be sure to safety-proof carefully and then, just for this time of life, provide access to as many of the cabinets, drawers, and pantry areas as you possibly can. Remember, it is not forever. At times, parents will show us a "safety-proofed" kitchen that features one or two cabinets for the baby and seven that are "off limits." In such cases, we gently explain to the parents that they've got it backward; the baby should have access to most of the cabinets, and the adults should be using very few during these months.

Kitchens are appealing because parents spend a lot of time there and also because babies absolutely crave access to cabinets. They love to swing doors back and forth. They love to get into the plastic containers and the pots and pans.

You should note that I encourage several child-rearing practices that involve a higher possibility of minor accidents than might otherwise occur. I urge the closely supervised use of a walker for the typical three-month period between four and one-half months of age and the onset of the crawling ability. I urge the limited use of a Jolly Jumper from four and one-half months until the baby becomes too heavy for the gadget, usually at about nine months of age. I strongly advise parents to safety-proof the home before the baby can crawl and then to allow her maximum access to explore, rather than make extensive use of a playpen or other practice designed to confine the child to a small space. I suggest allowing a baby unlimited opportunities to practice climbing the first two steps of a flight of stairs.

All these recommendations have something else in common. They represent what normal babies are particularly keen on doing at designated periods of life. They also provide substantial nourishment for the normal baby's initially strong interests in satisfying curiosity and mastering and enjoying motor activities. Not only does engaging in such activities help enormously to maintain the balance of primary interests and to avoid spoiling a child, but these activities are very useful practices in regard to first-rate, overall development during the early years, as you will learn from *The First Three Years of Life*.

Another classic threat to the maintenance of the balance among the major interests appears to be too much time spent with the mother. While it is certainly true that lots of mothers of infants are working part- or full-time out of the home these days, others are spending just about all their time at home with their babies throughout their child's first few years of life. Not only can that situation become surprisingly stressful, even when there is only one healthy baby at home, it also creates a higher risk of overdevelopment of orientation (overattachment) toward the mother than is desirable.

During a baby's first two years, whether substitute care is used or not, in virtually every instance the mother remains the principal emotional focus for the baby. It makes no difference whether it is your biological child or an adopted child. If, from the first months of life, the mother is the principal comforter, as is usually the case, she will come to have far more emotional clout with that baby than any other person in the world, even a full-time nanny. Even when the father becomes the principal caregiver during the first years, the mother remains the principal focus, except in rare instances. This is probably due to the fact that mothers and infants establish a very special bond during the baby's first months of life.

Especially in those instances when the child is not allowed maximum access to the home, full-time stay-at-home mothers tend to have babies who orient considerably more toward them than they should. The result often is a loss of the balance of primary interests. This is much less likely to happen if the mother is away from the baby regularly for several hours at a time.

I strongly recommend that you take time off from child-rearing responsibilities regularly between the baby's eighth and twenty-fourth months of life. I urge you to make use of teenagers or others who have the qualities that are necessary to babysit regularly during that period of time. We strongly recommend outings to the park, drop-in centers, and "fun" programs for babies, or even just walks. Again, the basis for these recommendations is the need to continue to feed effectively a child's curiosity and interest in doing things with her body.

Notice I haven't talked much about toys during this particularly important age range. Once crawling begins, very few toys will hold a baby's attention for long. A few do have considerable appeal, and I have written about them extensively. Compared with the opportunity to explore a home and practice crawling, pulling to stand, and cruising, however, they just can't compete.

## WHAT ABOUT GRANDPARENTS?

It is reasonably well known that grandparents are suckers for their grandchildren and notorious for overindulging them, but the impact of grandparents is not a major factor in determining whether or not a child becomes an unpleasant two-year-old. When you count the number of hours of contact that grandparents usually have with children and compare that with how much time parents spend with children, it becomes obvious that unless the circumstances are quite unusual, the likelihood of a major impact from overindulging grandparents is negligible. I suggest you relax and let grandparents and babies have their time together without interference. Obviously if the grandparents are the principal child-rearers, it's a whole different story.

## TRIPS—GO NOW, PAY LATER

From the time a baby is seven and one-half months old (and with some, even earlier) on through the second year of life, you can count on trips to produce disruption and complicate the socialization process. Most babies settle into a reasonably civilized pattern of sleep by six months of age. The most common pattern is: to bed between 7:00 and 9:00 P.M. and up in the morning between 5:00 and 7:00; two naps of an hour and one-half, one in late morning, the other in mid to late afternoon. I hasten to add that there are plenty of variations of this typical timetable by normal babies.

If your eight-month-old has settled into a regular pattern and you take her away for a week to visit family or have a vacation, you should be prepared for sleep disturbances for up to a week after you return home. We have found that from seven and one-half to twenty months or so, the duration of the sleep disturbance is directly dependent on the length of the trip. Even trips as short as a few days can be expected to be disruptive. You may now find the baby much less willing to take a nap. He may also stop sleeping through the night. Such behavior is perfectly normal, but unfortunately it happens often during the months when the child is experimenting with insisting on getting her own way. The same sort of complication arises from the common minor illnesses of infancy. It sometimes isn't easy to tell whether your baby is practicing powerful demanding or just feels rotten.

## THE EFFECTS OF A NANNY OR AN AU PAIR ON YOUR CHILD'S SOCIAL DEVELOPMENT

For any number of reasons, you may decide to make use of a nanny or an au pair. Such a decision can lead to substantial benefits for you, but it can also cause various degrees of grief. Much depends on how careful and fortunate you are in your choice. I hope you have become convinced that your baby's early experiences have a powerful influence on her development and her future. If you have, then clearly your goal should be to find someone who will do a great job.

I would suggest you keep the following factors in mind. Obviously you want someone who is warm, intelligent, and experienced. Training is usually, but not always, an asset, because first-rate training is scarce and common sense is more important.

You will need someone whose ideas about rearing a child are compatible with your own. Some experienced caregivers may hold rigid beliefs you won't be comfortable with. In fact, the more experienced a professional, the more likely this problem is. The person you hire may believe that a lot of comforting of your baby during his first months will spoil him. Or she may not be willing to let your ten-month-old "mess up" the kitchen by playing with the contents of the cabinets. Her ideas about discipline may be quite different from yours.

Since children learn about two-thirds of their basic language during the first three years, and since first-rate language learning during the early years is very important, you should pay particular attention to this subject. Many families use nannies or au pairs whose first language is not the same as theirs. Your nanny need not have outstanding language ability (in your language), but neither should she be inadequate in that respect.*

You should have assurance that your nanny or au pair will work for you for an appropriate length of time. The effects of a nanny's departure depend on how old the baby is at the time and how deep a relationship has formed. If the

---

*Babies are remarkably adept at acquiring more than one language during their first years. You might consider hiring someone in part to help your baby become bilingual. Linguists advise that if you do, you should have each adult use his best language consistently with the baby, rather than switch from one to another.

nanny has been with your baby for eight or nine hours a day for more than a few months during the seven- to twenty-four-month period, you can expect that a fairly strong tie has been established. Your baby will probably be very unhappy for several days after the nanny leaves. With extra attention from you, I would expect a return to normal within a week or so, and no long-term negative effects. On the other hand, if you have used a nanny full-time for a year or two from the time your baby was only a month or two old and she leaves, the effects will probably be serious.

The younger your baby is when you hire someone, the longer the commitment you need. If the baby is a newborn, I suggest two and one-half years. If the baby is eighteen months old, one year will do. Of course, you should aim for as long-term a commitment as you can get, but remember, you may get a long-term commitment with a nanny you discover is not right for your family.

## SOCIAL DEVELOPMENT AND HAPPINESS

I am sure you want your child to be happy just as much as you want her to grow up unspoiled. In the case of first children growing up in loving families, free from significant problems such as poor health or poverty, the process of socialization during the early years is intertwined with the evolution of happiness or its opposite. Put simply, a spoiled twenty-seven-month-old is invariably a chronically unhappy child, while an unspoiled twenty-seven-month-old is almost always full of joy. In this book, I have concentrated on the evolution of social interests, styles, and abilities, and made comments along the way about happiness or its absence. Here I want to make the picture about the evolution of happiness as clear as possible.

It is easy to identify when unhappiness begins. Surely it is reasonable to assume a newborn is unhappy when he is crying. It is not so easy to identify the first signs of happiness. Most people know what happiness looks like: smiling, laughter, and squeals of delight are pretty good indicators. Babies don't show many of those behaviors during the first ten weeks of life. Perhaps the closest a baby comes to happiness during those first weeks is when, her needs fulfilled, she appears to be comfortable. What can you do for her during those first weeks? Your job is to keep the inevitable periods of distress to a minimum.

During the period between the emergence of regular smiling (eight to twelve weeks) and the intentional cry (five and one-half to six months), you need to continue to head off and reduce discomfort, but you can also enhance happiness through both play and the provision of exciting things to do. Tha latter goal is easily achieved through the effective design of your baby's physical environment. So, for example, mirrors and hand-eye toys like the floor gym, along with toys to facilitate bouncing, clearly lead to lots of laughing and expressions of sheer delight by the middle of the fourth month.

These two tasks of the first six months—minimizing physically based discomfort (from hunger, gas, and illness) and providing opportunities for having fun—are required throughout the balance of the first three years. What does not begin during the first six months is your baby's unhappiness because of interpersonal experiences. One of the first signs of that new and important stage occurs when your baby pushes aside a spoonful of food while making a noise of objection in response to your feeding attempts. From that point forward, your socializing style will become the major factor in determining how happy your baby will be from day to day.

From seven and one-half to fourteen months, your success in setting limits and in teaching your child to take minor discomforts in stride will directly determine how happy your child will be as a fourteen-month-old. Ineffective limit setting and overreactions to minor mishaps produce fourteen-month-olds who cry a lot and often appear to be dissatisfied. Happiness at fourteen months depends largely on successful socialization in the preceding eight months of life. The chief difficulty for parents is that effective limit setting requires that at certain times a parent refuse to be swayed by a baby's cries of unhappiness. Paradoxically, the best long-term outcome requires parents to occasionally cause short-term unhappiness in their child.

The picture stays the same throughout the balance of the first twenty-two months. Some degrees of intermittent unhappiness, caused by your refusal to yield to his demands, simply has to happen for your child during the fourteen- to twenty-two-month "experimentation with power" period for the best long-term results. Under ideal conditions, such episodes begin to diminish by nineteen or twenty months and become quite rare after twenty-two months. If they become more frequent and intense after twenty-two months, the cause is inevitably inadequate limit setting.

It is truly remarkable how some babies from loving homes, having shown typical euphoric and endearing behavior when they were four months old, become chronic malcontents, full of complaints, by two years of age, while others become incredibly happy about their lot in life.

## A FINAL NOTE—BE CAUTIOUS

Because of breakthroughs in research on the subject since the late 1960s, our understanding of the details of early social development is much better today than it has ever been before. Nevertheless, it is still far from complete. Information about babies and how to raise them can be found in a huge number of books, in newspaper and magazine articles, and on radio and television programs, not to mention in tips from friends and relatives. Pity the poor person who tries to sort it all out on his own! I have long advocated help for new parents, particularly through programs like New Parents as Teachers.

You may have noted that some important social topics haven't been mentioned in this book. You've read little here about self-confidence, self-image, and self-respect, and only a modest amount, in the light of their importance, about the emotions. The reason for those omissions is not that I don't think such topics are important but rather that I don't believe there is enough known about them to warrant even speculation from me. I would feel uncomfortable making recommendations about them, even though, like anyone interested in babies, I have lots of hunches.

My advice to you is to be cautious. There is a lot of misinformation around, and there are a lot of questions that no one can yet answer. In general, you should adopt a skeptical attitude in the face of this situation because so much of what is offered is, unfortunately, not valid.

CHAPTER 7

# Concluding Remarks

FEW subjects are as exciting to me as the social development of a baby. It is an ever-rewarding experience to watch a baby evolve from a totally unknowing newborn to become a responsive, endearing five-month-old; to progress through the innocent social explorations of the seven- to twelve-month period to the tentative awareness of self and budding interpersonal power of the fifteen-month-old; and subsequently to undergo the somewhat arduous working through of the relationship with authority. What finally emerges is a remarkably complex, accomplished, and exciting individual at two years of age.

You have been through the process now, but as the baby's parent rather than as an observer. For you, the emotional impact of the day-to-day experiences, and especially the dramatic changes, has undoubtedly been great. Your role has been to provide the love that is essential for a solid, emotional beginning and to teach your child how to relate to people by showing her how to live in your family. I hope that the information in this book has helped you enjoy the experience even more than you otherwise would have. Furthermore, I hope it has helped you avoid much of the needless anxiety that often accompanies a parent's child-rearing efforts. And, of course, I hope the information has helped you do an effective job of giving your child a great start in life.

There is, of course, much ahead for you as a parent. Introduction to school, the perils of adolescence, and the concerns of the rest of your child's life that will inevitably be part of yours. But during these first years, you have had a very special role to play in building the foundations of your child's social and emotional life. If you have played this role well, you have taught your child the core lesson that he is loved, unique, and an extremely important person, but no more so than anyone else in the world. Nothing you do for him in the future will be more important for his happiness.

# Recommended Readings

A small number of books are of special value as you go about the task of raising a delightful child.

B. White, *The First Three Years of Life*. New York: Prentice Hall Press, 1991.

This book, which first appeared in 1975, is aimed at providing a comprehensive look at the early years of a baby's life from an educational perspective. It is designed to help you produce the most wonderful three-year-old you can. It is based on more than thirty-four years of continuous research on optimal development during the early years. Unlike the book you have just read, which is focused on socialization, it is designed to deal with all major developments, including mastery of the body; vision and hearing; intelligence and language; and a baby's rapidly shifting interests. It describes the month-to-month developments of all major abilities, normal variability, typical hazards to the best outcomes, and what seem to be the most effective parental practices.

J. Piaget, *The Origins of Intelligence in Children*. 2nd ed. New York: International Universities Press, 1952.

Without question, Piaget has been head and shoulders above the rest of the field with respect to new knowledge about how the intelligence of man develops. His writings are classics. In fact, there is no better original material than the work of this man to guide you to an understanding of how the mind of your baby functions. He was and remains the only true genius in this field.

Piaget's own writings are extremely difficult. Only a brave minority of academics read and use them. If you have trouble with his writings, I suggest you read the following excellent book by Singer and Revenson. Whichever readings you choose, if you learn from Piaget something of how your baby's mind functions during his first two years, you will enjoy your child even more, save yourself some occasional needless stress, and probably be aided measurably in your roles as your child's first teacher and pal.

D. Singer and T. Revenson. *Piaget Primer: How a Child Thinks.* New York: Plume Books, New American Library, 1978.

Dorothy G. Singer and her husband, Jerome, have been outstanding students of human development for more than twenty-five years. They are among a minority of writers who not only are very well informed but recognize what they don't know as well. This book by Ms. Singer and her associate T. Revenson will provide you with a much easier access to Piaget's ideas about how a young child's mind works than the original writings. I recommend it highly.

F. Maynard, *The Child Care Crisis.* New York: Penguin Books, 1986.

Substitute care for infants and toddlers remains a controversial and important subject. This author has written one of the most thoughtful and useful analyses of the subject. I think it is a very important book that ought to be read by anyone considering extensive use of substitute care during their child's first years.

R. Bush. *A Parent's Guide to Child Therapy*. New York: Delacorte Press, 1980.

If, as your child approaches her third birthday, you begin to feel dissatisfied with her social behavior (in spite of my book), you can expand your knowledge about what to be concerned about and what not to be concerned about by reading this book.

The author provides a remarkably rational and comprehensive introduction to the subject of child therapy. Witness, for example, the title of Part 1: "When, Where, and How to Get Help," a promise that Bush goes on to fulfill. The book is written in a realistic yet reassuring tone. The author reveals a rare degree of common sense and a capacity for dealing with the subject in a concise and accurate way.

# Index

accidents:
  safety-proofing of home and, 139–40, 227–28
  serious, 121, 173
  *see also* minor mishaps
achievement, showing pride in, 101, 103–4, 129
adolescence, 171
adoption, 221–22
adults, used as resources, 101, 103, 129
aggression, 36, 161, 164
anticipatory response, 55
attachment process, 36, 194, 198, 199
  imbalance among primary interests and, 168
  "overattachment" problems and, 44–45, 168
attention:
  crying in order to get, 65, 71, 73, 76–77, 78, 80, 82, 84, 88–89, 95, 128
  excessive demands for, 44, 59, 123, 155
  responding to overtures for, 149–50
au pairs, 231–33
  language skills of, 232
  time commitment of, 232–33
authority:
  of child over parent, 41
  child's acceptance of, 180

limit setting and, 147–48, 151–53, 185, 204, 234
testing of, *see* testing behavior
automobile rides, newborn comforted by, 69, 70

babies:
  bare feet recommended for, 91
  playing with other babies, 160–62
  premature, 134, 217–18
babies, from birth to five and one-half months, *see* newborns
babies, from five and one-half to seven and one-half months, 74–96
  boredom and frustration in, 80, 82, 84, 85, 95
  capabilities of, 80, 83
  curiosity of, 80, 83–84, 85–87, 88
  designing suitable environment for, 87–93
  emergence of capacity to complain in, 82–83
  goals for, 85
  intentional cry for company in, 76–77, 78, 80, 82, 84, 88–89, 95
  interests of, 87–88, 89–93, 95
  interpersonal development of, 98
  jumper-type toys for, 89–90, 228
  leg-muscle development in, 89–93, 95

babies, from five and one-half to
　　seven and one-half months,
　　*(cont.)*
　normal social development of,
　　74–83
　potential problems in, 83–84
　sleep patterns of, 93–94
　spoon feeding of, 77–78
　stranger anxiety in, 74–76
　walkers for, 90–93, 228
babies, from seven and one-half to
　　fourteen months, 97–157
　adults used as resources by, 101,
　　103, 129
　bad habits in, 116–17, 131,
　　143–47, 155
　balance among primary inter-
　　ests of, 139, 154–55
　boredom and frustration in, 128,
　　139
　crawling of, 105–7, 111, 120,
　　121, 123–29, 130, 139–42,
　　155–56
　crying after minor mishaps,
　　109–11, 112–13, 130–31, 142
　curiosity of, 111, 124, 128, 141
　development of social competen-
　　cies in, 101–4, 106
　development of social interest
　　in, 98–101, 102
　diapering of, 119–20, 148–49,
　　151–52
　dinnertime problems in, 133–34,
　　135–36
　feelings expressed by, 101, 103
　goals for, 138
　hand-eye skills of, 105, 111–14,
　　156
　imitation in, 104, 114–16, 153
　importance of social develop-
　　ment process in, 121–23
　initiating of games by, 117–18,
　　153–54
　insisting on getting own way,
　　117–20, 132–36, 147–48,
　　152–53, 155
　interpersonal development of,
　　126–27
　language abilities of, 136–37
　large-muscle skills of, 105–9,
　　141
　limits imposed on exploration of,
　　120, 121, 125–29, 154–55

　make-believe or pretend play of,
　　101, 104
　neglect of, 129
　normal social development of,
　　97–123
　offering explanations to, 136–37,
　　144
　potential problems in, 123–36
　pride shown in achievement by,
　　101, 103–4, 129
　responding to overtures of, 149–
　　150
　safety-proofing home for, 139–
　　140, 227–28
　separation anxiety in, 99, 131,
　　141
　setting limits with, 147–48,
　　151–53
　sibling rivalry in, 100–101, 123,
　　125
　sleep patterns of, 132–33, 150–
　　151
　spoon feeding of, 114
　stranger anxiety in, 98–99, 131,
　　141
　surrogate caregivers and, 120–
　　121, 141
　testing behavior of, 133
babies, from fourteen months to
　　twenty-two to thirty months,
　　158–96
　attachment process in, 194
　balance among primary interests
　　of, 168, 192–95
　balls and books appealing to,
　　159–60
　bullying behavior in, 161, 175–
　　179
　complaining of, 168–69
　consequences of poor socializa-
　　tion of, 179–80
　"directing" behavior of, 166–68
　emergence of self-awareness in,
　　170–71, 173
　exercise groups for, 195
　experimenting with power, 158,
　　160, 166, 169–72, 174, 182,
　　185–88, 194
　feelings expressed by, 165
　first lies of, 182–83
　goals for, 181–84
　interpersonal development of,
　　176–77

make-believe or pretend play of, 165

negativism in, 170–72, 173, 182, 196

normal social development of, 158–72

part-time vs. full-time parenting of, 194

peer interactions of, 160–62, 183–84

potential problems in, 173–81

prevention of proximity as control tactic for, 188–92

psychological testing of, 171–72

puzzles for, 192–93

recommendations for, 185–92

sibling rivalry in, 162–64

sleep patterns of, 175–78, 191

social lessons learned by, 172

television or videos and, 195

testing behavior of, 169–70, 171, 172, 173–75, 181–82, 185–88, 196

thinking abilities of, 182–83

"time out" procedure and, 190–191

babies, from twenty-two to thirty months to thirty-six months, 197–215

development of interest in people in, 198–201

direction of social interest in, 200–201, 209

feelings expressed by, 202–3

interpersonal development of, 210–13

language abilities of, 208–9

make-believe or pretend play of, 204

normal social development of, 197–209

nursery school experiences and, 214–15

pace of development in, 198

peer interactions of, 200, 201–4, 208, 209, 214–15

play groups for, 215

in power struggles with parents, 199, 204, 209

self-confidence of, 204–5

sibling rivalry in, 199–200, 206–207

testing behavior of, 205–9, 214

babysitters, 230

from seven and one-half to fourteen months, 120–21, 141

bad habits, 116–17

development of, 131

eliminating of, 145–47, 155

preventing development of, 143–44

balls, playing with, 159–60

bathrooms, safety-proofing and, 140

batting of objects, 52

bedtimes and nap times:

crying at, 93–94, 132–33, 150–151, 175–78, 191

procedures for, 150–51

bedtime stories, 94

behaviors, parents' reactions to, 89–90, 114, 115, 116–17, 143

bilingualism, 232n

birth order, 164

biting, 116, 143, 145, 163

books:

"directing" behavior and, 166–67

playing with, 160

boredom, 80, 82, 84, 85, 95, 128, 139

bouncing activities, 89–90, 156, 228

Bowlby, John, 62

breastfeeding, 94

Brookline Early Education Project (BEEP), 44

bullying, 161, 175–79

bumps and bruises, see minor mishaps

caregivers, substitute, 230

for babies from seven and one-half to fourteen months, 120–21, 141

for newborn, 63

Care of the Infant: Human and Animal, 222–24

Center for Parent Education (Waban, Mass.), 24–26, 45

child care, see day care

civil rights movement, 29

climbing, 168, 228

development of abilities in, 107, 108, 109

limiting toddler's natural interest in, 121, 168

minor mishaps and, 142

climbing *(cont.)*
  possibility of accidents in, 121
  safety-proofing of home and,
    139–40, 227
clingy behavior, 139, 159, 194
clothes, choosing of, 185
colic, 58, 70, 71–72, 82, 219–20
comforting:
  automobile rides in, 69, 70
  colicky babies and, 220
  cry-response-comfort cycle and,
    53–55, 57
  elevator move in, 68
  gentle movement through space
    in, 68
  after minor mishaps, 110–11,
    112–13, 130–31, 234–35
  pacifiers in, 67, 68, 70
  techniques for, 54, 66–71
  various sound patterns in, 69–70
complaining, 36, 168–69
  whining and, 37–38, 61, 139,
    173, 179, 194
conditioning, in newborn, 53, 55
confinement:
  to crib or playpen, 125, 128, 155,
    189–90
  exploration limited by, 120, 121,
    125–29, 154–55, 226
  restriction of movement disci-
    pline technique and, 145–46
  "time out" procedure and, 190–91
cradles, 68
crawling, 87, 96, 105–7, 111, 120,
    123–29, 139–42
  dangers posed by, 124–25
  delayed development of, 155–56
  limits on range of, 120, 121,
    125–29, 226
  minor mishaps and, 130, 142
  opening home to, 141, 226–29
  parental response to, 124–29
  safety-proofing home and,
    139–40, 227–28
creative activities, 204–5
cribs:
  automobile-ride simulators for,
    69, 70
  confinement to, 125, 128
crying:
  at bedtimes and nap times,
    93–94, 132–33, 150–51,
    175–78, 191

colic and, 58, 70, 71–72, 82, 219–
    220
comforting techniques and, 54,
    66–71
cry-response-comfort cycle and,
    53–55, 57
during diapering, 119
evolution of, 81
excessive, development of, 130–
    131
for help, 107–8
inconsolable, 54, 71–72
to insist on getting own way, 118,
    132–33
intentional cry for company and,
    65, 71, 73, 76–77, 78, 80, 82,
    84, 88–89, 95, 128
minor mishaps and, 109–11,
    112–13, 130–31, 155, 219
neglect and, 64
of newborn, 52, 53–55, 57, 59,
    64, 65–72, 73, 76–77, 130
parent's temperament and, 222
separation anxiety and, 99
spoon feeding and, 77–78
  *see also* tantrums
curiosity, 107, 167, 168, 178–79,
    218, 229, 230
  from five and one-half to seven
    and one-half months, 80,
    83–84, 85–87, 88
  hindrance of, 123
  of newborn, 65
  of newly crawling baby, 124,
    128
  from seven and one-half to four-
    teen months, 111, 124, 128,
    141

danger:
  potential for serious accidents
    and, 121, 173
  safety-proofing of home and,
    139–40, 227–28
  setting limits and, 151–52, 153
day care, 215
  at home, social isolation and,
    120–21
  for newborn, 63
diapering, 61, 97, 119–20, 148–49,
    151–52
  distraction tactic in, 119
digestive discomfort, *see* colic

dinnertime, 133–34
  "directing" behavior at, 135–36
  food dropping or throwing at,
    116, 144, 217–18
"directing" behavior, 117–18,
    134–35, 166–68, 203
  in book sessions, 166–67
  leadership with peers as out-
    growth of, 118, 166, 203
discipline, 27
  prevention of proximity in, 188–
    192
  restriction of movement in, 145–
    146
  "time out" in, 190–91

earrings, pulling on, 143
egocentric thinking, 33
ego psychology, 28
elevator move, 68
emotional development, first three
    years of life crucial in, 34–35
Erikson, Erik, 28, 58
exercise groups, 195
explanations, to babies from seven
    and one-half to fourteen
    months, 136–37, 144
exploration:
  limiting of opportunities for,
    120, 121, 125–29, 154–55, 226
  opening home to, 226–29
expression of feelings:
  from fourteen months to twenty-
    two to thirty months, 165
  from seven and one-half to four-
    teen months, 101, 103
  from twenty-two to thirty
    months to thirty-six months,
    202–3

faces:
  funny, 115–16, 117
  newborn's interest in, 50, 51
facial characteristics, stranger
    anxiety and, 75–76
falling, see minor mishaps
father, 172, 229
  temperament of, 225
feeding, 118
  intentional cry and, 77–78
  prematurity and, 217–18
  spoon, 77–78, 114, 234
  see also mealtimes

feelings, see expression of feelings
feet, bare, recommended for
    babies, 91
First Three Years of Life, The (tele-
    vision program), 43–44
First Three Years of Life, The
    (White), 17–18, 32, 42–43,
    100, 140, 149
five and one-half to seven and one-
    half months, see babies, from
    five and one-half to seven and
    one-half months
food dropping or throwing, 116,
    144, 217–18
fourteen months to twenty-two to
    thirty months, see babies,
    from fourteen months to
    twenty-two to thirty months
Freud, Sigmund, 28
friendships with peers, 183–84,
    200, 208
  see also peer interactions
frustration, 80, 82, 84, 85, 95, 125,
    139
full-time parents, 39, 141, 155
  overdevelopment of orientation
    toward, 229–30
  part-time parents vs., 194
funny faces, 115–16, 117

genetic defects, late parenting and,
    219
glasses, knocking off, 116, 143
grandparents, 40, 56, 230
group care, 215
guilt, of working mothers, 220–21
gumming, 80, 88, 95, 116, 160

hair pulling, 116, 143, 144, 145,
    163
hand-eye skills, 80, 88, 95, 218
  puzzles and, 193
  from seven and one-half to four-
    teen months, 105, 111–14, 156
happiness, social development
    and, 146–47, 233–35
Harvard Preschool Project, 17, 28,
    30–39, 44
  conclusions of, 36–39, 41–42
  first three years of life as focus
    of, 33–35
  observation methods of, 33,
    35–36

Harvard Preschool Project *(cont.)*
  well-developed six-year-olds
    described by, 30–32
head butting, 116, 143
Headstart, 29
health concerns, 216–20
  chronic illness and, 219
  late parenting and, 218–19
  prematurity and, 134, 217–18
  prolonged colic, 219–20
"healthy selfishness," 43–44, 150,
    152, 222
hearing, 80, 83
helplessness, of newborn, 52–53, 56
hitting, 116
Hodgson-White, Janet, 68
humor, 208

illness, chronic, 219
imitation:
  in newborn, 115
  from seven and one-half to four-
    teen months, 104, 114–16,
    153
immobilization, in elimination of
    bad habits, 145–46
infant seats, 87–88
initiating of games, 117–18, 153–
    154, 166, 167, 203
intelligence, development of, 198,
    218
intelligence tests, 34
intentional behavior, first, 77
intentional cry:
  for company, 65, 71, 73, 76–77,
    78, 80, 82, 84, 88–89, 95, 128
  spoon feeding and, 77–78
interest in people:
  clingy behavior and, 159, 194
  from five and one-half to seven
    and one-half months, 74–76
  from fourteen months to twenty-
    two to thirty months, 159–
    164
  in newborn, 50–51
  playing with other babies and,
    160–62, 180, 183–84, 200,
    201–4, 208, 209, 214–15
  separation anxiety and, 99, 131,
    141
  from seven and one-half to four-
    teen months, 98–101, 102,
    131, 123–24, 129

stranger anxiety and, 74–76,
    98–99, 131, 141, 159
  from twenty-two to thirty
    months to thirty-six months,
    198–201
  *see also* sibling rivalry
interpersonal development:
  from five and one-half to seven
    and one-half months, 98
  from fourteen months to twenty-
    two to thirty months, 176–77
  in newborn, 60
  from seven and one-half to four-
    teen months, 126–27
  from twenty-two to thirty
    months to thirty-six months,
    210–13
interviews, in research, 26–27, 35

jumper-type toys, 89–90, 156, 228

kitchen:
  baby's exploration of, 227–28
  safety-proofing of, 140, 227–28

laboratory sessions, 35
language abilities, 34, 165, 183, 198
  futile explanations and, 136–37
  nannies or au pairs and, 232
  responsive style and, 149–50
  from seven and one-half to four-
    teen months, 136–37
  from twenty-two to thirty
    months to thirty-six months,
    208–9
  understanding meaning of "no"
    and, 143
language tests, 34
large-muscle skills, 105–9, 141
  crying for help and, 107–8
  leg-muscle development and,
    89–93, 95
  minor mishaps and, 109–11,
    112–13
  sitting position and, 85, 92, 105
  standing position and, 89, 107–8
  *see also* climbing; crawling;
    motor development; walking
late parenting, 218–19
leadership with peers, 202, 203–4
  "directing" behavior as precur-
    sor of, 118, 166, 203
learning, capacity for, 53, 55, 107

newborn's capacity for, 53, 55
leg extension reflex, 89
leg muscles, development of, 89–93, 95
limit setting, 185, 204, 234
  from seven and one-half to fourteen months, 147–48, 151–153
  taking baby's point of view into account in, 151–53
love, unconditional, 65
lying, 182–83

make-believe or pretend play:
  from fourteen months to twenty-two to thirty months, 165
  from seven and one-half to fourteen months, 101, 104
  from twenty-two to thirty months to thirty-six months, 204
manipulative skills, 37–38, 61
Maslow, Abraham, 28, 30
maternal-deprivation studies, 62–63
mealtimes:
  dropping or throwing food at, 116, 144, 217–18
  prematurity and, 217–18
  resistance to spoon feeding and, 77–78, 114, 234
memory, development of, 198
mental abilities, 35, 182–83, 198, 208–9, 218
minor mishaps:
  crying after, 109–11, 112–13, 130–31, 155, 219
  parental reactions to, 110–11, 112–13, 130–31, 234–35
Missouri Department of Education, 44
mother:
  excessive orientation toward, 124, 129, 155, 201
  temperament of, 225
  too much time spent with, 229–30
  working, guilt of, 220–21
motor development, 105–9, 229
  crying for help and, 107–8
  from five and one-half to seven and one-half months, 89–93, 95

minor mishaps and, 109–11, 112–13, 130–31, 155, 219
  from seven and one-half to fourteen months, 105–9
  see also climbing; crawling; walking
Murphy, Lois, 30

nannies, 231–33
  language skills of, 232
  time commitment of, 232–33
naps, see bedtimes and nap times
nature vs. nurture, 98
negativism, 38, 40–41, 170–72, 173, 182, 196
neglect, 129
newborns (from birth to five and one-half months), 49–73
  attractiveness of, 56, 75
  colic in, 58, 70, 71–72, 219–20
  comforting techniques for, 54, 66–71
  crying of, 52, 53–55, 57, 59, 64, 65–72, 73, 76–77, 130
  curiosity of, 65
  designing suitable environment for, 234
  emergence of intentional cry in, 65, 71, 73
  emergence of social awareness in, 51
  having fun with, 72–73, 234
  helplessness of, 52–53, 56
  imitation in, 115
  interest in other people developed in, 50–51
  interests of, 87
  interpersonal development of, 60
  learning of, 53, 55
  maternal-deprivation studies on, 62–63
  neglected, 64
  normal social development of, 49–59, 60
  pace of development in, 79
  prematurity and, 217
  signs of happiness in, 233–34
  sleep patterns of, 50, 66, 79
  smiling of, 50, 51, 55–56, 59, 64, 73, 234
  social goals for, 65
  special concerns about health of, 216–20

newborns *(cont.)*
   substitute caregivers and, 63
   trust in people developed in, 58
New Parents as Teachers program
   (NPAT), 18, 21, 44–46, 225,
   236
"no," understanding of word, 143
nursery monitors, 175
nursery schools, 202, 214–15

observation method, 33, 35–36,
   46–47
   quantitative approach and,
   46–47
"observer effect," 26
orphanages, 64, 99
"overattachment" problems, 44–45,
   168
overindulging, *see* spoiling and
   overindulging

pacifiers, 39–40, 54, 64, 68, 70
pain, crying as response to, 53,
   109–11, 112–13
parenting:
   approaches to study of, 26–27,
   35
   best practices in, 42
   "healthy selfishness" in, 43–44,
   150, 152, 222
   late, 218–19
   parent's temperament and,
   222–26
   part- vs. full-time, 194
   sources of information on,
   23–26, 46, 235–36
   stressfulness of, 38–39, 72
   *see also specific topics*
parents:
   reactions of, to baby's behavior,
   89–90, 114, 115, 116–17, 143
   *see also* father; mother
*Parent's Guide to the First Three
   Years of Life, A* (White), 18
parent support groups, 225
part-time parenting, 194
patty-cake, 115, 153, 166
pediatricians, as sources of information on parenting, 24
peek-a-boo, 115, 153, 166
peer interactions, 180
   bullying behavior in, 161

expression of feelings in, 202–3
   from fourteen months to twenty-
   two to thirty months, 160–62,
   183–84
   leadership and, 118, 166, 202,
   203–4
   nursery school and, 214–15
   play groups and, 215
   from twenty-two to thirty
   months to thirty-six months,
   200, 201–4, 208, 209, 214–15
personality:
   development of, 22–23, 59, 98
   inborn factors in, 22–23, 59, 98
   nature vs. nurture debate and,
   98
   stability of, 205
Piaget, Jean, 23*n*, 33, 35, 52, 56,
   77, 170, 178, 182, 218
Plato, 27
play:
   with agemates, *see* peer interactions
   with balls, 159–60
   with books, 160
   "directing" behavior in, 117–18,
   166–68, 203
   initiating of games in, 117–18,
   153– 54, 166, 167, 203
   with puzzles, 192–93
   with toys, 114, 128, 155, 156, 230
play groups, 202, 215
playpen, confinement to, 125, 128,
   155, 189–90
pop-up toys, 114, 156
power struggles:
   from fourteen months to twenty-
   two to thirty months, 158,
   160, 166, 169–72, 174, 182,
   185–88, 194
   play with peers as version of,
   204
   from twenty-two to thirty
   months to thirty-six months,
   199, 204, 209
   *see also* testing behavior
prematurity, 134, 217–18
preschool programs, 29, 214–15
Preschool Project, *see* Harvard
   Preschool Project
pretend play, *see* make-believe or
   pretend play

prevention of proximity, 188–92
  "time out" vs., 190–91
pride, in achievement, 101, 103–4,
  129
problem solving, 77
process monitoring, 35
Project Headstart, 29
psychological testing, 171–72
psychology, 28
"pushy" behavior, see "directing"
  behavior
puzzles, 192–93

questionnaires, 26–27

reading to child, 166–67
reason, appeals to, 190
reasoning abilities, 198
recognition of special people, 55
reflexive responses, in newborn,
  52
restriction of movement, in elimination of bad habits, 145–46
rocking chairs, 68

safety-proofing home, 139–40,
  227–28
scolding, 131
 self-assertion, 41
self-awareness, emergence of,
  170–71, 173
self-confidence, 204–5
sensory development, 50, 80, 83
separation anxiety, 99, 131, 141
Sesame Street, 29
setting limits, see limit setting
seven and one-half to fourteen
  months, see babies, from sev-
  en and one-half to fourteen
  months
sharing, 208
sibling rivalry, 37
  from fourteen months to twenty-two to thirty months, 162–
  164
  interviewing parents about, 27
  onset of crawling and, 125
  from seven and one-half to fourteen months, 100–101, 123,
  125
  spacing of children and, 37, 42,
  184, 206–7

from twenty-two to thirty
  months to thirty-six months,
  199–200, 206–7
siblings, 61
  age gap between, 37, 39, 42, 164,
  184, 206–7
sitting position, 85, 92, 105
six-year-old, competent or well-
  developed, 30–32, 33, 64–65
sleep:
  bedtime or nap time procedures
  and, 150–51
  from five and one-half to seven
  and one-half months, 93–94
  from fourteen months to twenty-
  two to thirty months, 175–78,
  191
  of newborn, 50, 66, 79
  from seven and one-half to fourteen months, 132–33, 150–51
sleep disturbances, 175–78, 191
  trips and, 231
SleepEase, 69
sleep signs, 93, 94, 132, 150
smiling, of newborn, 50, 51, 55–56,
  59, 64, 73, 234
social awareness, emergence of,
  51
social development:
  from birth to five and one-half
  months, 49–73
  checkpoints in, 59–61
  early conclusions about, 36–42
  first three years of life crucial in,
  34–35
  from five and one-half to seven
  and one-half months, 74–96
  from fourteen months to twenty-
  two to thirty months, 158–96
  happiness and, 146–47, 233–35
  quantitative research on, 46–47
  from seven and one-half to fourteen months, 97–157
  from twenty-two to thirty
  months to thirty-six months,
  197–215
  see also specific topics
socialized thinking, 33
sound patterns, newborn comforted by, 69
spanking, 42–43, 146, 208
Spitz, René, 62

spoiling and overindulging, 37,
    40–41, 45, 73, 83, 134–36
  neglect and, 64
  origins of, 85, 95
  undoing effects of, 209
spoon feeding, 114, 234
  intentional cry and, 77–78
stairs:
  climbing up and down, 107, 108,
    109, 227, 228
  safety-proofing of, 140
standing position, 89, 107–8
stories:
  bedtime, 94
  make-believe, 165
stranger anxiety:
  facial characteristics and, 75–76
  from five and one-half to seven
    and one-half months, 74–76
  from fourteen months to twenty-
    two to thirty months, 159
  from seven and one-half to four-
    teen months, 98–99, 131, 141
sucking urge, 53, 54, 88
Sullivan, Harry Stack, 28
survey methods, 26–27
swings, 68

taking turns, 168, 203, 204, 208
talking, 170, 183
tantrums, 23, 36, 37, 41, 61, 155,
    191, 194, 209
  *see also* crying
Taubman, Bruce, 70
Tavistock Clinic, 55
teething, 82, 116
television, 27, 195
"terrible twos," 18–19, 21–23,
    36–37, 41, 61, 182, 209
testing behavior, 41
  close spacing of children and,
    206–7
  from fourteen months to twenty-
    two to thirty months, 169–70,
    171, 172, 173–75, 181–82,
    185–88, 196
  prevention of proximity and,
    188–92
  in pursuit of learning, 185–88
  receding of, 205–6, 208–9, 214
  from seven and one-half to four-
    teen months, 133

from twenty-two to thirty
    months to thirty-six months,
    205–9, 214
thinking, 182–83, 198, 208–9, 218
  egocentric vs. socialized, 33
  emergence of ability in, 35
three-year-olds:
  characteristics of outstanding
    six-year-old found in, 33–34
  intelligence and language abili-
    ties of, 34
tickles, 51
"time outs," 190–91
toddlers, *see* babies, from fourteen
    months to twenty-two to thir-
    ty months
toilet training, 40, 171
Tors, Ivan, 222
touch, 51
toys, 128, 155, 230
  balls, 159–60
  pop-up, 114, 156
trips, sleep disturbance and, 231
trust in people, emergence of, 58
twenty-two to thirty months to
    thirty-six months, *see* babies,
    from twenty-two to thirty
    months to thirty-six months
two-year-olds:
  unpleasant behavior of, 18–19,
    21–23, 36–37, 40–41, 59–62,
    181–82, 206, 209
  well-developed, 36, 37
  *see also* babies, from twenty-two
    to thirty months to thirty-six
    months; "terrible twos"

verbal abilities, *see* language abili-
    ties; talking
verbal scolding, 131
videos, 195
visual abilities, 50, 80, 83

walkers, 90–93, 156, 228
  objects hung from, 91
  safety precautions for, 90–91,
    92–93
walking:
  "cruising" as precursor of, 108–
    109
  minor mishaps and, 109–11,
    112–13

timing of first unassisted steps
    and, 109
waving bye-bye, 115, 153
Westinghouse Corporation, 43
whining, 37–38, 61, 139, 173, 179,
    194

White, Robert, 28
*Why Is My Baby Crying?* (Taubman), 70
working mothers, guilt of, 220–221
World Health Organization, 62